WHAT WAR COULD NOT DESTROY

TWO SOLDIERS, ONE DIARY, AND CROSSING FROM WAR TO PEACE

PAUL REED

HIS Publishing Group is a division of Human Improvement Specialists, llc.

For information visit www.hispubg.com or contact publisher at info@hispubg.com

Front cover images inspired by Colin Kimball and Danny Burks.

ISBN: 979-8-9905246-2-0 *paperback*

What War Could Not Destroy

A small handwritten diary kept by a North Vietnamese soldier, later captured by an American soldier, becomes an unexpected bridge between two former enemies—opening a path toward understanding, reconciliation, and healing from a war neither of them fully understood.—Provided by the Publisher

1. Vietnam War 2. Reconciliation/Forgiveness 3. Healing

Printed in the United States of America

Division of Human Improvement Specialists, llc.
www.hispubg.com | *info@hispubg.com*

CONTENTS

ACKNOWLEDGMENTS

As with all stories of war and healing, this one did not end with a final scene or last embrace. Life went on for those who lived it—and so did the memory of those who passed. What follows is not a list of names ... but the final chords in a long, soulful melody.

POLLY BAKER (PAUL'S MOTHER)

Polly was the one who reunited me with the diary—that was tucked away in a box in her attic. Long before I understood its power, she had insight into its purpose. Without her urging to get it translated, the love Nghia had for his wife, family, and country might never have been revealed. And the friendship between him and me might never have happened. Polly passed away in early 2003.

LEO BAKER (PAUL'S FATHER)

He was a quiet man, a petroleum engineer, who loved fishing. On a trip together, he told me he didn't care what I became—only that I be the best at whatever it was. We often disagreed, but before he died, he admitted he never realized how deeply the war had damaged me until he saw me wrestle through the aftermath. He was moved by the journey Nghia's little diary took me on—and the fact that Nghia became one of my best friends. Leo passed away in early 2004.

SILAS BAKER (PAUL'S SON)

His birth was a miracle. The doctors insisted he was a girl, due to the sonogram, but my prayers were for a boy. And that's what I told them he'd be. Today, Silas lives near Dallas and directs physician recruitment for a healthcare firm. He's the devoted husband and father of two wonderful boys—my grandsons, ages eleven and almost ten. Though I was distant early in his life due to the trauma the war created, we've grown very close. We are now best friends, like two men in scripture—Paul and Silas.

LUONG THANH NGHI (THE TRANSLATOR)

Nghi rose from the Ministry of Foreign Affairs to become Vietnam's ambassador to Australia. Despite his demanding schedule, he still visits and sends occasional emails. During my last visit to Hanoi, he greeted me warmly and called me a celebrity. "That can't be true," I said. "Oh, but it is," he replied. "I've seen you on TV at least ten times." Our friendship continues.

VU THI GAI (NGHIA'S WIFE)

She once told her husband that both he and the little book she gave him would return to her after the war. The book's presence was steady, as though it waited to be opened when the time was right—miraculously, it found its way home along with its owner, fulfilling Vu's prophecy. She was one of eleven children; nine of her siblings died of starvation during the Japanese occupation of WWII. She passed away in 2008.

LT. NGUYEN VAN NGHIA

A commissioned officer in the People's Army of Vietnam, Nghia served with the 24th Regiment of the elite 304th Division—one of the most storied combat formations of the war. He walked the length of the Trường Sơn corridor, commonly known as the Ho Chi Minh Trail, fought in the Central Highlands, and endured nearly losing a leg along with other near-fatal wounds that should have ended his life, but didn't. Instead, he survived and returned home to further his boyhood skills in poetry, to be a father, a husband, and a revered elder in Thai Binh.

After the death of his beloved wife, he said life felt lonely—but he remained grateful for the bond we had built. Nghia lived to the age of ninety-six and passed in early 2025. To me, he was more than a former enemy. He was my brother-in-arms. He once told me he would not be the man he is today if we had not met. On another occasion, a friend asked if he truly believed Paul Reed cared for him. Nghia smiled and replied, "He has come to see me more than nine times already." His words crossed a war, an ocean, and his life crossed a century, and his heart crossed an enemy.

PAUL REED

I raised my son, Silas, as a single father, and I am now the proud grandfather of two boys, ages ten (almost) and eleven. I discovered that writing—and speaking—could be a powerful balm for pain. Along with fellow US Army veteran Ralph Gillum, I co-founded the *HerdHistoryProject.com*, a site for our 173rd Airborne brothers-in-arms to share and preserve their combat experiences. My mission today is simple—to speak of peace, and to bear witness to reconciliation. I speak about forgiveness because that's where true inner healing begins. When we forgive, we're not saying what happened to us was okay—instead, we are letting go of the pain that had been controlling us.

STEVE SMITH

Steve served two tours in Vietnam with the Marine Corps before graduating from Oregon State University. He became a television journalist and then an award-winning documentarian, producing over 200 films and earning four Emmy nominations and sixteen Telly Awards. He was the one who saw something in this story before anyone else did.

PHIL STURHOLM

Phil filmed over 50 hours of footage documenting the friendship between Nghia and me. A decorated Army veteran and gifted cameraman, he won more than 30 Emmy Awards and was inducted into the prestigious Silver Circle. Phil passed away in 2016.

THE DIARY

The little book that connected enemies, softened hearts, and bridged nations eventually disappeared. Nghia lost it on a train in North Vietnam. When I heard the news, I didn't feel sadness—only awe. "It served its purpose," I said. "It did the work it was supposed to do... and then moved on." I like to think its power lives on, somewhere else now, doing what it was always meant to do. More than a diary of words from the past, it was a passageway toward healing for people who still needed it.

MEDIA & DOCUMENTARY COVERAGE

This story has been documented across national and international platforms over the years. While this book remains the most complete and personal account of the journey, the following programs and publications offer additional perspectives on the events described within these pages.

FILM & TELEVISION

PBS—*Kontum Diary* (Emmy Award-Winning Documentary), a feature-length documentary chronicling the return of Nguyen Van Nghia's diary and the unfolding journey of reconciliation between two former enemies. Broadcast nationally and internationally.

CBS News—*48 Hours: The Fight to Forgive, a* nationally broadcast segment highlighting the transformation from battlefield enemies to friends, with emphasis on forgiveness and healing.

NBC—*Today Show* (Live National Interview) Bryant Gumbel interviewed Paul Reed regarding the return of Nguyen Van Nghia's wartime diary and the unlikely friendship that followed. The nationally televised segment reached an estimated audience of more than 30 million viewers.

ABC's Channel 8 News—Good Morning Texas Show, a live interview with Nguyen Van Nghia and Paul Reed at Belo Broadcasting's *Channel 8 Studio* in Dallas, Texas, discussing Nghia's trip to the U.S. from Vietnam for treatment of his war wounds and the friendship that developed between the two former war combatants.

National Press People Magazine—December 16, 1996—*Men at Peace*, a national feature article exploring the reconciliation between two former combatants and the human story behind the diary.

More information is available on the project's official website, www.thediarybridge.com, which serves as a continually expanding historical archive of the diary's journey and its enduring impact. There are additional interviews, articles, broadcasts, and archival materials, including extended footage and rare historical documents.

PREFACE

I shouldered the shotgun. "Back off!" I shouted. "Get out of the way, Peacemaker—I'm gonna blow his head off!"

Peacemaker looked up, saw the barrel, and lunged at me. "No! Don't do it! You'll kill him—we'll all go to jail!"

We hit the pavement, wrestling for the gun. I barely noticed the passing cars, but I heard tires squeal when drivers saw two truckers fighting in the middle of the interstate, and one of them was holding a shotgun.

That is one of many events in my life post-Vietnam. Like most soldiers who fought in that war, part of me stayed there—never came home. This book is not a war story or a story about death or dying on the battlefield; it's about the journey I took to find my way home and, in doing so, helping others find their way home as well, regardless of what war or circumstance they have experienced.

My journey centers on a small book I captured during combat—hidden away for nearly two decades—that opened a path for me and led to the life I live today. The small journal was more than words—it carried the voice of an enemy soldier who, like me, had been called into battle. His words, his poetry, his longing for love and peace reached across oceans, across decades of silence, but most importantly, across cultures, traditions, language, beliefs, and distortions of truth.

But in my story, his small book became the catalyst that connected us, brought about changes between us, and enabled us to form a life-long bond and lives of peace. Finally, but probably most importantly, I realized that God sometimes places the smallest things in our hands to lead us toward forgiveness, a healed heart, and the ability to love others as we love ourselves.

FOREWORD

If someone had told me that a small, hand-written diary—taken from the jungle floor of Vietnam—would one day become the bridge between two former enemies, I might have laughed, or worse, turned away.

At the time, I was a young paratrooper in the 173rd Airborne Brigade, hardened by combat and hollowed by the ugliness of war and death I'd seen and experienced. We had been trained to see the enemy as less than human—an image burned deep into our minds long before the first shot was fired. The war left its marks on all of us—scars that went deeper than any wound a bullet could make. For years after coming home, I tried to live as if the war had ended, but inside me, it never did.

Then one ordinary day, my mother brought down from the attic a small C-ration box that had been sitting quietly, unnoticed and forgotten for two decades. Inside was something I had long forgotten, a captured diary belonging to an enemy soldier I'd once fought against. The handwriting was delicate, the most beautiful I had ever seen. I couldn't read the words, as they were Vietnamese, but something about them reached out to me, as if they had something to say. That diary, sent home as nothing more than a souvenir of war, became the most *momentous item of substance* I ever brought back from Vietnam, causing flowers to again bloom in the killing fields.

What happened next was not a coincidence—it was calling. The diary led me on a journey I could never have imagined: a journey to find the man who wrote it, Nguyen Van Nghia. Against every odd, we found one another—two soldiers from opposite sides of the same war—and together we discovered that forgiveness could grow out of even the darkest soil. Standing with Nghia, face to face, I came to understand that the truest victories in life aren't won on battlefields, but in the human heart.

This book, *What War Could Not Destroy*, is the continuation and completion of that journey—the full story of how a forgotten artifact of war became a vessel of peace, how pain became purpose, and how two men learned to see each other not as enemies, but as brothers. It is not only about Vietnam, but about every person who has ever carried the weight of hatred, loss, or guilt—and wondered if healing was still possible.

I wrote this book so that anyone who opens its pages might find something of their own reflection inside. Maybe you've fought a war of your own—with an employer, with a neighbor, a former wife or husband, a stranger, or even within yourself. My hope is that *What War Could Not Destroy* will remind you that even from the ashes of suffering, grace can rise.

The small box that once held a captured diary now holds something greater, a message that forgiveness is stronger than fear, and love is more enduring than war.

—*Paul Reed*, Texas, 2026

CHAPTER ONE

WYOMING

A convoy of three tractor-trailers rolled south on old Highway 30, hauling Washington apples bound for Texas. I was in the lead truck, thirty-something and sleep-deprived, running on nerves and caffeine.

"Ridge Runner, you copy?" came the voice over the CB.

It was Bubba Swearingen or Peacemaker, as he was known on the CB.

"Watch your speed. Speed trap ahead."

"Copy that," I said. "But this isn't bear hours. We've got to be in Texas by tomorrow afternoon."

Paul Reed standing in front of the truck he drove for James Young Trucking.

We pulled into the Kemmerer, Wyoming, port of entry. Peacemaker, Dennis Williams (CW handle on CB), and I went inside to get our logs checked. The officer behind the desk moved like a sloth in molasses. I took the chance to hit the restroom.

When I came back, my buddies were already gone. A stranger from another rig stood next in line, logbook in hand. Without thinking, I cut in front of him and slapped my logbook onto the counter. The guy shot me a look that said everything.

The officer time-stamped my book, and I hustled out. I was barely back on the two-lane road when I spotted the stranger's Freightliner in the rear-view, closing in. He moved to pass, but oncoming cars blocked the lane. I shifted to the shoulder to give him room, but he just hovered there, crowding my mirrors. I keyed the mic.

"If you're gonna pass, pass. I'm not staying out here all day."

There was no response.

Then, without warning, he pulled out into the left lane. There was a car coming fast.

This should've been the moment where I backed off—let him in, avoid a pileup. But I didn't. I stayed pedal to the metal, adrenaline pumping, heart locked in that cold, narrow place I knew too well.

We were neck-and-neck when he gave me the finger. Then his trailer cut inches in front of me, swerving hard. I hit the brakes. If I hadn't, I'd have ended up upside down in the ditch. In the rearview, the car he nearly hit had flipped—tires in the air, a dust cloud rising behind it.

I could've let it go. Maybe I should have. But I couldn't. Something inside me snapped, and in that instant, a cold fear crept up my spine—not of him, but of myself. My hands trembled, my chest was tight, and suddenly I couldn't breathe. My mind was no longer on the highway.

I was back in Vietnam in Kontum Province—March 1968

My hands gripped the wheel tightly, but my vision blurred.

The jungle reeked of rot and sweat. We'd been pushing along a ridgeline west of Dak To, sweeping narrow trails the NVA used to flank our outposts. Everything was too quiet, like the trees were holding their breath.

Then the point man and first one behind him took rounds and were down. We hit the dirt hard. Sitrep from point element came back two were down, not moving. I could smell powder, blood, and jungle heat all mixed together.

Blackshear and Tremblay took rounds to the head—no warning, just gone. They had to lie where they fell because the enemy had us pinned down. I remember trying not to breathe too loud, afraid even the air might give me away.

As the sun went down, we were still stuck to the ground. But as darkness crawled in, sniper fire faded just enough for us to break contact and slip back to our night defensive position, or

NDP. I was soaking wet with sweat and urine, and tried to sleep, but thoughts of Tremblay and Blackshear lying dead, where they fell, made sleep almost impossible.

That kind of fear doesn't leave you. It just waits inside, quiet, like something crouched in the tall grass—until the next time you need it.

And now, only a few years after returning home from some of the most vicious, anger-filled, kill-or-be-killed combat war had ever produced, on a sunbaked highway in Wyoming, that same fear—that was a heart-ripper—was back in charge.

The CB crackled, "Peacemaker, CW—do you copy?"

Their voices came through—steady, calm—but I wasn't.

I told them what happened. Every word burned through my teeth. The flipped car. The Freightliner that nearly killed me. The silence. The finger. They didn't hesitate. We bunched up, four trucks tight and fast, tail-to-nose down the highway like a rolling wall of steel.

The stranger must've realized what was coming. He peeled off onto the Salt Lake exit, thinking he'd throw us off.

"Let him go," Peacemaker said. "We've got a deadline."

But I couldn't shake it. My hands were still shaking. My jaw was clenched so hard it felt like it might snap.

"It's not over," I said.

We stopped in Green River to grab coffee, but my mind wasn't there. I barely tasted it. I barely spoke. My heart was still pounding, like the firefight hadn't ended yet.

Fifteen minutes later, we were back on the road. I took the point again. As we rounded a wide curve, a lone truck crept out from a business access ramp onto the interstate ahead, going east-bound, same as us.

At first, it didn't register, but as we closed in, the shape, the chrome, the markings—it all clicked. It was him the same Peterbilt. The driver had hoped to fool us by taking the Salt Lake City exit earlier off Old Highway 30, just before reaching the eastbound entrance to I-80, that led to Laramie, but he had taken his first exit off I-80 going west and did a U-turn back east toward Green River. Thought he could ghost us.

Not today. That boil in my chest came back. But this time it wasn't just anger. It was fear turned inside out. It was survival instinct—raw and irrational—firing on all cylinders. I down-shifted, boxed him in. He swerved right, then left, looking for an out. I keyed the mic.

"I got you now, driver. I got you now."

For ten minutes, we locked him in, four semis pressing like a vise. Every second, my foot got heavier. My blood got hotter. Finally, I braked hard. All four rigs squealed to a stop smack dab in the middle of Interstate 80.

I didn't think. I just moved. I grabbed the sawed-off from behind my seat, jumped down, and charged the back of my trailer. He'd stopped just short of rear-ending me. Peacemaker was already pulling him out of his cab by the leg.

I shouldered the shotgun. "Back off!" I shouted. "Get out of the way, Peacemaker—I'm gonna blow his head off!"

Peacemaker looked up, saw the barrel, and lunged at me. "No! Don't do it! You'll kill him—we'll all go to jail!"

We hit the pavement, wrestling for the gun. I barely noticed the passing cars, but I heard tires squeal when drivers saw two truckers fighting in the middle of the Interstate—one of them holding a shotgun.

The stranger in the Pererbilt floored his rig and took off, engine howling as he escaped.

CW shouted, "He's getting away, y'all!"

I didn't chase him. I didn't say a word as I made my way back to my truck.

But anger was burned deep in my soul, and I was ready to inflict violence on the enemy, just as the enemy in the jungle. And what scared me most wasn't what almost happened. It was knowing I wouldn't have stopped myself.

CHAPTER TWO

FORT POLK

When I was young, my father assured me that I would be provided with the necessities of life: food, clothing, education, and a roof over my head until I turned 18 and longer if I went to college. Additionally, he informed me that anything beyond those essentials—including unnecessary things I merely wanted or desired—would not be paid for by him.

Not long after that conversation, I decided I could earn about $20 a month by cutting grass. It pleased me to have my own money, and it was even more rewarding to see the approval on my father's face.

After a summer or two of mowing lawns, a route manager for the Dallas Times Herald offered me an afternoon paper route.

"There are about forty customers," he said. "If you've got a bicycle, it'll go fast."

I delivered papers for about a year—on a bicycle my father had given me to get to school. At the corner where trucks dropped bundles of paper, there were two or three other boys with bikes—and one with a motorcycle. A Honda.

Not long after I started, Tony Middleton, the boy with the motorcycle, said he'd be glad to help me throw my route if I helped with his.

“Both routes could be thrown in the same time as one—with this,” he said, pointing at the Honda.

Nine months later, I set my sights on owning a motorcycle. But I was only thirteen.

“Don’t forget,” my father said, “I’m providing the necessary things—and a motorcycle is not one of them.”

A year later, just days before my fourteenth birthday, I took delivery of a brand-new Honda from Britton Motorcycles on Maple Ave in Dallas, a nifty-difty-thrifty Honda 50. My dad had come around—he agreed to pay half, so long as I managed to save the other half of the $275 cost, which I somehow did.

Now, with my own motorcycle, I found others in my school who had them too, like the twin Messina brothers, Tom and John, who lived three streets over.

One sunny afternoon, the three of us approached a footbridge near our houses that crossed a creek. The twins watched as I gunned my motor and began across the narrow bridge. It was meant for foot traffic only, so it was no surprise when I wound up in the creek bed below—knocked smooth out, on top of jagged rocks. Water flowed over me as I lay unconscious, coming to with one twin on each side, frantically yelling for me to wake up.

My head felt foggy, as if waking from a very deep sleep. A gaping hole above my right eye—caused by smashing into a rock—bled heavily. The twins, panicked, got me onto the buddy seat of one of their bikes, and as I held my head in both hands, we took off. Within minutes, I stood—barely—on my doorstep, blood running down my face, all over my shirt. When my mother opened the door, her face turned pale, and she almost fainted, but somehow, she reached for me as I wobbled forward and got me inside to a chair.

Three different motorcycles and three serious wrecks later, our next-door neighbor, Brendan, came home on leave from Germany. He had joined the Army the year before and became a

U.S. paratrooper, now stationed overseas. I stared at his photos, trying to imagine what it was like to jump out of airplanes.

"Could it be worse," I asked him, "than several motorcycle wrecks and smashing into rocks at the bottom of creeks?"

He laughed, then showed me something even crazier. Behind John J. Pershing, the elementary school I'd attended through sixth grade, several older boys had rigged a form of parasailing. They tied a WWII surplus parachute to the rear bumper of a pickup truck using a hundred-foot rope. Any kid willing to take the risk got a turn.

When one of the guys with the pickup said, "Who's next?" I raised my hand. The first few seconds were uneventful. The pickup rolled forward slowly, and I had to sprint after it faster and faster until the chute behind caught wind—taking me up, up, up!

As long as the truck kept moving, keeping the chute in the air, I floated along on an unbelievably smooth ride, fresh air hitting me in the face, enjoying the most joyous ride of my life.

But soon I would realize the ride would end. After a minute or two, the driver slammed on the brakes, allowing the chute I was dangling below to descend toward the earth. I'd had no training and no instructions on how to land. I was on my own, and landing safely depended largely on one's instinct. When I hit the ground, I felt like I'd just discovered a new calling. I understood at that point what Brendan had said about hitting the ground. I was hooked.

Extracurricular thrills excited me more than high school ever did. I didn't grasp how important education was—or that it was the groundwork for my entire life. That mindset led me to enroll in a course called Distributive Education. The deal was simple—keep passing grades and hold a job for a set number of hours. I was good with that.

One day in high school, I told my counselor I wanted to learn Spanish.

"That's a wonderful goal," she said. Then she went to retrieve my file.

When she returned, she looked at me sympathetically. "It's an honorable thing, learning a new language," she said, "but you have to pass English first."

John F. Kennedy had inspired millions with his speech, "Ask not what your country can do for you, but what you can do for your country." At the time, I didn't fully grasp what Kennedy meant, but as I got older, it influenced me more. A year later, I approached my father and told him I wanted to join the Army. I wanted to be a paratrooper like Brendan.

I had experienced parachutes, wind in my face, and a growing sense of purpose. I'd seen soldiers on the Nightly News—fighting in a jungle, in a place called Vietnam, no one had ever heard of, far from home. I never told my dad directly that my intention was to be a warrior like those I saw on TV.

In 1965—the war became my calling.

At seventeen, I was ready. School wasn't my strength, but I believed I could master something else—something bigger. I told my father so. He sat reading a book as I spoke, pretending not to listen—but he heard every word. He had high hopes for me: college, a career, grandchildren. When I finally said the word "fighting," he closed his book, looked me in the eye, and said, "What exactly is it you need from me?"

"A signature," I said. "I'm only seventeen."

His answer came quick and flat. "No. You'll get your diploma first. After that, you'll be eighteen. Then you can do as you please."

One day, I straddled my motorcycle outside the steps of my high school, revved the engine, and popped the clutch. I blasted up the stairs, through the main hallway, laughing, wild, unstoppable. My joyride came to a sudden end when I nearly ran over the principal, who was waiting at the far end of the hallway. When I got home early, my mother asked why.

"I got expelled," I said. "Three days."

"That means you'll miss finals," she snapped. "And if you don't take those, you'll be back again next year."

She said, "Get in the car." Once there, she marched me into the principal's office.

"If my son doesn't take his finals," she said, "he'll be back here next year."

The principal's face went pale at the thought of my return. He agreed.

Mr. Sam Godfrey, my geography teacher, agreed to pass me if I earned it. He sat me in a corner, not facing the class, and told me to write an essay on everything I knew about a car, from bumper to bumper. I wrote what I knew. The paper earned me an A+. It raised my failing grades just enough.

When I walked into the Army recruiting office, on my face was a grin from ear to ear. All I could think about was the thrill of jumping out of airplanes, the fun of it all, pay was just a bonus. The danger of jumping from a plane while it was in flight never crossed my mind. I wasn't worried about dying. I wasn't even thinking about getting hurt.

Staff Sergeant Russell fit my image of what a paratrooper should be: tall, lean, hard-cut, clean-shaven, and squared away. Regulation crew cut. Khaki uniform. Confident posture. He knew just what to say. He talked about how elite the Airborne was, how a man could aspire no higher than to become an Infantry paratrooper. How tough the training would be. He looked me over like he was sizing me up and down.

Then he said, "You might have what it takes."

That was all I needed to hear, even though I weighed only 139 pounds soaking wet. I signed the paperwork that day—no hesitation. I was told to report for a physical exam the next day. Once cleared, I'd have 24 hours to pack.

That next day, when Staff Sergeant Russell, who was standing by the green army bus door, called my name out of about twenty to thirty guys, I hollered "Present!" and stepped onto the bus.

I was headed to Fort Polk, Louisiana.

CHAPTER THREE

NGUYEN VAN NGHIA

Nguyen Van Nghia was born in North Vietnam on August 10, 1928, in Tay Giang village, part of Tien Hai district in Thai Binh province, near the Red River Delta, not far from the harbor at Haiphong. His parents, poor rice farmers, died while he was still a young boy.

He was taken in by his aunt and uncle, who raised him as their own. There was no dentist in the village—no clinic, no hospital—but Nghia never needed one. By some twist of fate, his teeth remained perfect. He never once had a cavity.

The boy was fed, clothed, and educated by his relatives. He could read and write by the age of four. Arithmetic came just as easily. He grew up on a steady diet of rice, fish, discipline, and love for his country. His aunt and uncle taught him kindness, pride in his heritage, and a duty to serve others. He never forgot it.

As a child, he was sharp, quick-witted, and unusually good-humored for someone who'd seen so much loss. He liked to laugh and liked even more to make others laugh. One day in high school, after returning from lunch, he slipped a small lizard onto a girl's shoulder while she sat at her desk. She didn't notice it until it crawled down her blouse, and then the room erupted in laughter.

She jumped, screamed, danced in circles trying to get it out, while the class howled so hard they almost came to tears. The teacher didn't need to ask who the culprit was. Nghia sat in the back, grinning from ear to ear.

Sometimes his uncle would take him into town. Once, they stopped at the local blacksmith's shop so Nghia could see how their garden tools were made. The memory stuck with him—the glowing furnace, the clang of steel, the girl who worked beside it. It inspired a poem—one of many he would come to write.

THE BLACKSMITH GIRL

I look up at the tall furnace
Welding fire brighter than the stars;
I look up at the tall furnace
And see the blacksmith girl
Looking up at the stars.

Daily she returns home, satchel in hand,
To enjoy a pleasant afternoon,
Still doting on her blacksmith mentor.
See her watch the flowers bloom in the
morning,
So absorbed in the moment;
She must be scolded by Mom.

Brilliant flames well constantly from the depths
Of her soul.
These find the tall furnace,
Stoking the welding fire to be brighter than the stars
That the blacksmith girl has fixed her eyes on.

She admires the stars as she does the fine
welding line

That she so loves.
Day after day, the girl's hands are busy,
For every tomorrow the furnace
yields a fresh batch of steel.

She feels happy, watching the country grow
stronger,
Flourishing like the morning blooms.
At exam time, the girl is a bouquet of fresh roses.
The tall furnace makes the future as bright
As the countless stars.

Instead of being condemned to the same grinding poverty his parents had known, Nghia was given a future. His school, like many others in rural Vietnam, was simple—a single room, wooden benches, dusty floors—but it was enough. He studied reading, writing, and *the operation*, the Vietnamese name for basic arithmetic.

He excelled. At 17, around the time World War II ended, Nghia joined the army. His brothers were scattered. His parents were long gone. He hadn't yet met his wife. There was only service. He fought the French in the northern provinces and later trained as a political instructor as the American War unfolded.

On one mission, he lost a front tooth. They were resting on the side of a hill, drinking from bamboo tubes. A soldier in front of him fell backward unexpectedly, and the end of the tube smashed into Nghia's mouth. The tooth snapped clean and nearly went down his throat. It was a small injury in the long list of things he carried.

War frightened him—but it didn't shake his resolve. He thought often of past generations—of centuries of resistance, of families who had fought and died to free their land from foreign rule. Nghia believed it didn't matter if he lived or died, so long as he served with honor.

In 1957, he married. He returned to farming—the same backbreaking labor that had taken his parents. But life held new meaning now. He had a wife. Soon, four children. His first son was born in 1959.

CHAPTER FOUR

CHERRY HILL

A military vehicle sped through the villages of Thai Binh Province, loudspeakers blaring. "Troops are needed. We must run the American invaders out and reunify the country."

When Nghia heard the message, he began discussing the situation with his wife. With the French defeat at Dien Bien Phu in 1954, Nghia's country faced a new threat—the Americans. From their dinner tables and shops, villagers listened as Hanoi's voice filled the air. The message was clear—war had returned. And with it, a call to patriotism.

Thai Binh, a province about seventy miles southeast of Hanoi, was a logical place to broadcast that message. More military-aged men lived there than in any other part of North Vietnam. Nguyen Van Nghia, a veteran serving in the army during the French occupation, chose to fight again when he heard the appeal. A respected man in his village, known for his poetry, his peace, and his quiet presence—Nghia was looked upon as an uncle figure by many.

But he had seen too much foreign occupation in his lifetime. The French had come in 1890 and had been run out, and now the Americans had come to replace them. And just like before with the French, they, too, would be driven out.

Nghia, already a survivor of one war, answered his nation's call to fight in another.

In 1965, the war became his calling. Later, he entered the military academy in the north and was commissioned as a second lieutenant in the 304th Division of the People's Army of Vietnam (PAVN)—an elite formation, among the earliest regular divisions of the PAVN, and one repeatedly assigned to decisive campaigns. Their specialty was maneuver warfare—stealth, discipline, and ambush.

His unit would face some of the most brutal fighting against American and South Vietnamese forces, operating far from home under conditions that meant survival was never guaranteed and dismemberment was common.

Nghia carried marching song cards and wrote poetry in a small book his wife had given him the night before his departure to the southern battlefield. Their route south wound through the Trường Sơn mountain range—what Americans called the Ho Chi Minh Trail. In that little book, he wrote of love for his wife and children, and of his commitment to fight to the last drop of blood for his country. At times, he would read those words aloud to his fellow soldiers, reminding them why they endured hunger, sickness, and the endless walking.

But when the column stretched thin and silence settled over the jungle, he whispered the words to himself. Through rain-soaked valleys, leech-filled ravines, and mountains that seemed without end, he carried more than ammunition. He carried memory. He carried love.

And somewhere along that long, wet corridor of sweat, blood, and poetry, Nguyễn Văn Nghĩa turned forty years old.

Now, after four months walking and sometimes riding in overcrowded vehicles with troops deep within the Truong Son mountain range, Nghia and his unit had reached their destination, previously mapped out by higher command in the south.

He was a newly commissioned 2nd Lieutenant in the People's Army of Vietnam. He was not among the conscripts sent to wander. These were men trained for decisive ground battles and ambushes—capable of delivering maximum damage to the enemy.

There were a few trucks. No trains. No ships. The journey was made mostly on foot. Each man carried enormous loads—backpacks full of supplies, weapons, and ammo. Hands blistered from carrying extra ammo, shovels, and picks. Their feet were shredded from walking miles in sandals made from old truck tires, cut to fit their feet, and held in place with pieces of an inner tube strapped around their ankles and across their toes. Sleep came in minutes, not hours.

Nghia gave some thought to their journey from Thai Binh. He recalled steep terrain, thick jungle, and visible animals, including many poisonous snakes. Hardwood trees stretched close to forty meters high into the sky, their canopies woven so tightly that not a single beam of sunlight broke through.

Maps confirmed their location—the northwestern corner of Kontum Province, a stone's throw to the tri-border of Laos, Cambodia, and Vietnam.

Death, dysentery, and desertion often overwhelmed his mind. Some of the horrors the younger soldiers found themselves in caused them to run, but the Tigers lurking in close proximity found them. What remained of them was buried in unmarked graves, only to melt into the forest floor.

There was never enough food, water, medicine, or rest. Never enough of anything. Everything became a threat—the enemy in the air and on the ground. Hunger. Tigers. Chemical defoliants. Poisonous snakes. Leeches. Malaria-carrying mosquitoes. Treacherous elevations. Suffocating heat. Torrential rains. Sharp rocks. Exhaustion. Sometimes, the worst enemy was time itself.

Their mission in the south was clear—ambushes. In preparing to ambush the Americans, they needed an initial defensive position. Their commander studied the maps and selected a stretch of high ground, deeply forested, overlooking a vast valley. It was concealed, elevated, and surrounded by natural barriers.

Old French maps identified the elevation as 1,064 meters—just over 3,000 feet. Nghia nodded when he saw the site.

"A perfect location," he told the company commander.

They began digging. Bunkers were constructed by platoon. Nghia oversaw placement and structure, while other officers mapped exit strategies and fallback plans. They adopted a name for the hill. It became *Cherry Hill*—in honor of comrades who had bled and died nearby, in a battle known to the Americans as the *Battle of Dak To*, not but a few hundred meters from where they were standing.

A recon team, including Nghia, was sent out to identify and establish a secondary position in case they needed to evacuate, due to the Americans overrunning them, or an artillery attack during the night. They returned hours later.

"An excellent site," Nghia said, pointing to the map. "A little over three hundred meters from here. Wedged between two mountains. Thick tree cover. And a mountain stream of fresh water running through it."

The commander nodded, "Does it provide cover from the air?"

"Yes, sir. The canopy is so dense that even the sun doesn't get through. No smoke would rise from our fires. The Americans won't see a thing."

"Good. If they come too close, we'll make them think we've vacated our current position. But in truth, we'll relocate to your recommended site and live to fight again."

The commander then gave Nghia direct orders.

"Lieutenant Nghia, your team will lead the entire company to our new diversionary location—so every platoon member can learn the trail—coming and going—like the backs of their hands. Set up hammocks. Designate ammo, medical storage, cooking, and equipment storage areas, and survey areas for placement of stairs on inclines if needed. Keep it disciplined and tight. When the site is secure, return for further instruction. Understood?"

"Yes, sir," Nghia and his men replied.

Then the commander added, "Take a stopwatch and time the round trip. We need to know exactly how long evacuation takes in the event of an artillery strike—or worse, an enemy infantry breach. Is that clear?"

"Yes, sir."

After the men ate rice and nuoc mam, the commander gathered the soldiers. Holding a newspaper at arm's length, he addressed them with a proud, steady voice. "This came from our political officer. Inside is a letter from President Ho Chi Minh—sent to Chairman Nguyen Huu Tho of the Southern Liberation Front. I want to read it to you. It will remind you why you're here, why you are far away from your homes, and why we sacrifice."

The commander scanned the circle of faces and began:

> *Dear Mr. Lawyer Nguyen Huu Tho, the chairman and many high-ranking men in the South Vietnam liberation group and soldiers,*
>
> *While our soldiers and civilians of two regions are continuously collecting many, many victories against Americans to get our freedom, the liberation of South Vietnam declared in large numbers to fight the American and South Vietnamese soldiers to the last drop of blood.*
>
> *We have had seven years of guidance from our clever southern liberation leaders and hero soldiers. We fought together bravely and destroyed many plans of the enemy; we have killed more than a million Americans and their*

allies. The Americans have been crushed and destroyed everywhere. With the momentum of our victories, the soldiers and people of South Vietnam rose up and attacked everywhere.

They fought in high spirit and created so much confusion for the army of South Vietnam. Our ancestors and people are proud of our heroes.

Because the Americans were crushed in many battles, they went crazy and started battles everywhere. They flew and bombed North Vietnam. The Americans have a big mouth and lie. They say they want a cease-fire and peace but continue shelling and bombing, but that won't stop our people from fighting. The lying won't stop our people. We will fight until our enemies leave our land. Together we're strong and will survive.

Our goals and our strategy is to fight the Americans and liberate South Vietnam. We work and fight together with the liberation army in our country and also outside our country with many of our friends and allies of the world and even anti-war American supporters.

We will beat strong and evil America. We will beat them with our high spirit fighting and united people—our soldiers and people of the south liberation group are together and brave. We keep up our high spirit with millions of people of South Vietnam.

We will succeed and bring peace for the entire country from north to south. We will not stop fighting the Americans. Seventeen million people of the north will support the fighting and produce our sources for our brothers and sisters in the south.

Together we are strong and sure of victory. One day our entire country will be united. North and south together we celebrate.

I am taking this time to get my thoughts to our seniors and soldiers, soldiers' mothers, and all brave south liberation people and kids. A big hug and kiss.

Finally, to our chairman and south liberation leaders after the victory.

—Ho Chi Minh, Hanoi 6/9/1967

CHAPTER FIVE

WELCOME TO VIETNAM

The following five parts unfold in a sequence that sometimes moves forward, sometimes backward, and at times back-to-back.

It was Jeffrey Ratzlaff, a friend of mine from the United States, who gave me my first glimpse of Vietnam. He and I were friends back home, and we often had common interests. He had been there for about six months. His uniform appeared old, torn, and soiled, as if it had never been washed—described, as I'd learn later, as needing its oil changed. His boots, no longer black, looked like cracked, brown, rough-out leather.

Dark circles under his eyes revealed he needed rest and real nutrition. He looked older than his years, much older than I remembered from our days at home. Still, Ratzlaff looked healthier than the second man I met that day.

The second man approached, his eyes apparently drawn to the silver wings on my uniform. His unit patch showed he'd served with the 173rd Airborne Brigade. He wanted to know which unit the new paratrooper in starched khakis and bloused jump boots was assigned to. When I said, "The 173rd," he froze. Then his eyes widened, locking onto something far away only he could see.

After a few moments, he dropped that distant stare and leaned in nose to nose and grunted, "I just hope you like killin', boy."

I answered softly, "Oh yeah? Why's that?"

"Cause you'll get to do plenty where you're headed."

PART 1

In the Central Highlands near Pleiku, I found my battalion's HHQ tent. The XO—our executive officer—looked me over as soon as I stepped inside and, after checking some paperwork, assigned me to Alpha Company, 1st Battalion, 503rd Parachute Infantry Regiment, one of the four infantry battalions in the 173rd.

"Your company's in Kontum," the XO said, moving toward the tent's opening, motioning for me to follow. Outside, he pointed toward a runway made of PSP (perforated steel plates). "Get yourself over there as soon as possible. When a Caribou with tail number A-374 lands, you get on it. And don't miss your flight."

Alpha Company had gotten the word. They were to rendezvous with me as soon as I deplaned. I stood on the PSP runway watching the plane disappear, wondering what was next. No horns. No kids playing. No ice-cream trucks jingling in the distance.

This wasn't any neighborhood I'd ever known. And then it hit me.

I was alone.

In all of my nineteen years, I had never been this alone.

It was scorching heat, jungle in every direction, black rain clouds swelling and ready to burst wide open, and men with rifles, grenades, and knives strapped on them everywhere waiting in the distance for me—battle-hardened troopers, sitting in silence, measuring the clean-shaven, cleanly dressed, green new guy who had just entered their war.

Alpha Company, First Battalion 503rd Parachute Infantry Regiment, February 1968. Captain Davis, Company Commander (CO), back row, far left.

After linking up with Alpha Company, we moved a few clicks to an obscure outpost called Poli Klang. The Special Forces camp was one of twenty-six scattered along the western Vietnamese border, running north to south about a click east of Laos and Cambodia, better known as the tri-border area. The one I'd just arrived at was one of only two in Kontum Province. It sat on slightly higher ground than the neighboring tri-border area to the west and offered a clear view of the Truong Son Mountain range—nicknamed the Ho Chi Minh Trail by the Americans—less than a click away.

Indigenous fighters, who often served alongside us and actually held us in higher regard than most Vietnamese people, had killed a wild hog. It was their way of showing hospitality—a home-cooked meal for the Americans in camp. I watched one of them carve a wild hog into pieces, then looked up and smiled at me like he was proud of the feast. I forced a smile, nodded like I was onboard, then quietly slipped away and went for C-rations instead.

The next morning, I stood facing west toward the mountainous trail, its valleys bristling with pathways running north and south, east and west, with some vanishing into the southern provinces—especially where I was. Then I heard the sound—a low, rolling boom, like thunder clawing its way out of the earth. I froze, eyes lifting to the horizon, waiting for storm clouds. But the sky was stripped bare, an unnerving blue. Not a cloud anywhere. And somewhere inside, I already knew—this wasn't thunder.

Suddenly, at eye level, in the direction of the trail, I spotted a line of clouds—like the trail of dust behind a speeding pickup truck on a powdery road. But these weren't white. They were thick, grimy, gray-colored clouds, rolling fast and billowing upward into the sky. North Vietnamese troops rushing along the trail couldn't hear the B-52s flying five or six miles overhead—but when the 750-pound bombs hit, the ground beneath me shook, and sounded like thunder. You could feel them more than a click away.

That was my first introduction to what became known as Rolling Thunder. I didn't need to be any closer to know entire enemy units hauling supplies south were getting vaporized—the clouds were changing colors—from gray to blood red.

Not more than two days at Poli Klang, company platoon leaders were dispatched by Captain Jim Davis and briefed on a new search-and-destroy mission he had received. PAVN troops had built a bunker complex high on a ridge overlooking the valley, close to the tri-border area by a couple of clicks.

Davis relayed the information he'd received from S-2 to the lieutenants that the enemy unit occupying the bunkers was the 304th PAVN Regiment out of Thai Binh Province in North Vietnam, adding a measure of warning—their specialty was ambushes. He closed the briefing by showing the lieutenants the enemy's location on the map, atop a ridgeline at an elevation of 1,064 meters.

That afternoon, Alpha Company boarded helicopters for a heli-borne combat assault. I heard someone mutter they hoped the LZ would be cold—a term I'd heard since arriving in Vietnam but still didn't fully understand.

Choppers dropped over ninety-plus of us, five to six hundred meters away from the pinpointed enemy bunker complex.

I slipped off the chopper floor into the heat, my boots hitting the ground hard, instinct taking over before thought could catch up. The smell of the jungle wrapped around us—wet earth, rot, and something else you could never quite name.

From the valley, where the choppers let us off, we could see the top of the over 3,000-foot elevation ridgeline, which became Hill 1064.

We moved out quickly, spreading into formation, each man locking into his place. Eyes scanning. Weapons ready. Every sense tuned to the possibility of contact.

Later that afternoon, after we'd swept the immediate area for well-used foot trails and obvious signs of the enemy—such as foxholes, firing lanes, and snipers in trees—Captain Davis spotted an ideal location for an NDP (night defensive perimeter) and ordered us to dig in. Foxholes dug were spaced ten to fifteen meters apart, forming a tight circular shape, and the CP (command post) was dead center inside the perimeter.

PART 2

Early one morning, while most in his company ate rice, Lieutenant Nguyen Van Nghia sat atop a bunker on Hill 1064, overlooking the valley below. From his vantage point, he watched helicopters disgorging American troops onto the valley floor—no more than 600 meters to his front.

Seconds later, the radio came alive with a warning edged in urgency: "Enemy forces entered U.S. Special Forces camp at Poli Klang forty-eight hours ago. Last confirmed sighting—173rd Airborne elements. Now moving toward your position. Contact likely. Prepare. Stay alert."

Nghia lowered the handset slowly, his eyes never leaving the valley. *173rd Airborne.* The name settled in his chest with weight. He'd heard of them only a couple months earlier at Dak To. These were not irregular forces. Not militia. These were trained paratroopers—disciplined, aggressive, relentless.

He studied the movement below---the spacing, the direction, the purpose. They were coming. Not by chance. Not wandering. They were moving with intent… straight toward his position.

Six hundred meters of jungle and heat lay between them. And closing.

Somewhere within that formation below, young paratroopers moved with purpose, unaware they were already being watched.

He had read about the Battle of Ia Drang—near Pleiku, not far away—and how the American First Cavalry Division used flying machines, but he'd never seen or heard them.

Official army word for People's Army units like his was, "Do not be alarmed," as a victory against the American units using the flying machines was not only likely, but probable. Still, watching American paratroopers from Alpha company spill out five to six hundred meters to his front was anything but comforting.

Before reporting what he had just seen, he recalled what other PAVN units had said about fighting Americans with helicopters at Ia Drang. They said, "When you go south to fight the enemy, never forget you will be fighting invaders. They have enslaved your southern brothers and sisters and must be kicked out of the land. Take his food. Use his weapons. Remember, if you kill, he is dead, but if you wound, you will take two or three out of the fight. Stalk silently, attack from cover, and in small groups. If you see you cannot win, leave quickly, do not fight, and do not be afraid of the flying machines. They only carry troops that can die from bullets."

"Come in, Lieutenant Nghia," the commander said from his underground office with a loud voice.

The lieutenant climbed his way down, snapping a salute while saying, "Lieutenant Nguyen Van Nghia reporting as ordered, sir," holding his salute until it was returned.

"Ah, Lieutenant Nghia. I sent for you because I was looking over our bunker complex last evening and noticed it needs better concealment, better camouflage. I want our position to be impossible for the Americans to find. Because of your expertise and knowledge in concealment, we established a diversionary position we can withdraw to in an emergency, should the enemy send artillery or try to overrun us, and that is good. But still, I have a hunch the Americans will be arriving at this area soon, and I want our positions not to be easily found."

They locked eyes and held the silence, when the commander heard Nghia say, "They are already here, sir."

Once the commander shook off what he'd just heard, he asked, "What unit do you believe the Americans have sent to meet their death?"

Nghia responded with the intelligence he had just received over the radio. They are believed to be the 173rd Airborne Brigade, our intelligence said sir, though in my opinion they could be the U.S. Army's First Cavalry Division."

"Why is that, Lieutenant Nghia?" the commander asked.

"Because that unit used the flying machines in the Battle of Ia Drang, and these soldiers have all come in helicopters as well, sir."

"Very well," the commander said. "We will give them the fight they are looking for, whatever unit they are."

Nghia saluted his commander and left.

He assembled his sniper team while keeping one eye on the valley and the other watching a large monkey spring from limb to limb. In the distance, he heard bombs exploding. American B-52s were dropping bombs on the trail he and his unit traveled not long ago. He flashed back to the sight of his PAVN brothers and sisters vanishing under B-52 bombs. He had to shake off the images.

He thought to himself, *Go home, Yankees, to your families, so I can go home to mine. I never wanted to fight you in the first place. I'm tired of fighting in a war that we will never let you win anyway.*

Later, the snipers that had been sent to fend off any American intruders in an ambush returned. "Report your successes to the commander," Lieutenant Nghia told them after he'd learned they had some kills.

"Corporal Quynh, regimental sniper, reporting as ordered, sir. We killed two Americans today."

The commander replied that he'd heard a lot of firing from M-16s. As they spoke, the commander sought information on where exactly they were seen. "How far from our position did you locate the Americans?" he asked.

"We first noticed their point element and another close behind him at about 500 to 650 meters to our west. Behind those, spread out and stretching all the way down the incline nearly to the valley, appeared at least a hundred more. The two we killed were within 350 meters of our main bunker complex here."

Others behind them moved forward and tried dragging away the bodies, but our continuous firing kept them pinned down, and by nightfall, they left. We got these things from their pockets," they said as they handed them over to their commander.

"This stuff is in English. I can't read it." Ah-ha! Now he understood Hanoi's wisdom in sending translators with the units.

"Go get Corporal Hung. This stuff is all in English." "Yes, sir."

As Hung climbed down into the commander's office, he said he was reporting as ordered.

"Where did you learn to speak English, Corporal?"

"In Washington, D.C., at the University of America," he said, taking the items the commander handed him.

Corporal Hung looked them over. "An unsent letter and two military ID cards," he said.

"Very interesting," the commander noted. "Please tell me what names are on the ID cards."

"Yes, sir," said Corporal Hung. He paused, sounding out the names as best he could. "Tremblay, Patrick J., and Blackshear, James G."

"What about the letter, Hung?"

"The letter is addressed to America, sir. It has a return address name and unit... Blackshear, James G., Alpha Company, First Battalion, 503rd Infantry, 173rd Airborne Brigade, APO, SF 96250... whatever that means, sir."

"Ah ha", he roared, before dismissing the snipers, Lieutenant Nghia was correct. It is the 173rd Airborne who have come to meet their deaths, and not the US First Cavalry.

As the day made its way toward evening, Lieutenant Nghia scanned the valley to their west. He saw no movement, but there was a breeze, and outstretched tree limbs blowing in the gust. It was not much, but it reminded him of home, of his family, and his beautiful young wife, Vu.

He removed the mud-caked little book from his backpack, as though it was waiting to be retrieved when the time was right—and, today, he told himself, he would write something—a remembrance of home. It went like this:

RETURNING NORTH TO VISIT HOME

The dirt road leading home is
vermilion red, ablaze like my soul.

The echo of peoples' voices resounds from the
empty ferryboat
as the pigeons' coo lengthens.

But the little book of the moment is lost in a
homeland that stays divided
in the heart of a separated lover
who grieves for his broken country.

One day of love spared for the motherland
is worth a hundred years remembering
the roof on one's home.

Wind teases the green rice seedlings.

Corn on the hillside sways gently in the breeze.

The banyan tree in the front of the coffee
shop recalls the days when I was young.

The mossy lake with the long bridge
recalls the evenings spent fishing.

Thatched cottages, bordered by areca and
bamboo, line the banks—
along with jackfruit and banana trees.

When he finished, Nghia sat still for a while, letting the words he wrote comfort him with happiness and satisfaction.

Later that same day, Nghia got permission to make another short trip to their diversionary camp, where, according to unit SOP, everyone except officers had stored their backpacks.

The lone sentry allowed him in after he gave the password, and Nghia stacked his pack among the others neatly lined by the stream. Combat with the Americans could erupt at any time, and he didn't want to lose the little book Vu had given him, so he was confident leaving it in their diversionary camp was the safest place for it.

He inserted the little diary in a thin, almost-transparent plastic bag, with the few other things he wanted to keep dry, tucked them deep inside the pack, and pressed it down as though planting a seedling into the earth. To Nghia, it was only a precaution.

What he could not have known was that in that gesture, he was also planting Vu's dream—her quiet prophecy of safety—into the soil of time, where it would wait in the dark until the day it got watered, to begin its growth back to her.

He patted the top of his backpack once, gently, as if saying goodbye, then reported his arrival to the commanding officer once he'd returned to their main battle position atop the summit of Hill 1064.

He had barely reported back to the commander when the air itself changed. The jungle seemed to hold its breath. Then a mortar round slammed into the hill to his front and exploded—so close it rattled the earth under his boots. Twenty-five meters to their front, dirt and fire leapt skyward, along with the acute, bone-shattering sound high-explosive mortar rounds make when they explode.

"It came from over there," one of the line soldiers shouted, pointing southwest. The soldier couldn't have known for certain what unit fired it, but in the jungle, mortars came faceless, echoes bouncing off the hills until no man could swear their source.

However, Nghia felt it deep in his chest—the rounds were coming from the paratroopers.

Another round followed. Then another.

The earth convulsed. Smoke billowed, screams broke loose.

"Our mortar crew," the commander screamed from his bunker below, "get me our mortar crew immediately."

"Sergeant Cho reporting, sir."

"Sergeant Cho, you are to make sure your gun is zeroed here," the commander said, showing him the spot on a map.

"Lieutenant Nghia," he shouted seconds before returning to his office underground, "make sure men are okay in their bunkers."

Before Nghia could say he'd comply with the commander's orders, another mortar round slammed in and exploded nearby. This one, the concussion, caused his ears to become moist—blood was coming out. He stumbled, fighting to stay upright, his mind caught between the blast and the thought of what he had placed earlier in his backpack by the stream. Vu's little book. Her prophecy. Safe for now—if only he could survive.

Both surprised and shocked by a much closer mortar round—he wasted no time feeling his way toward the closest tunnel for safety. Just as he was about to enter, another round came smashing in—this one a direct hit to the cache holding their mortars—causing a huge explosion—as Nghia's ears bled, the world around him a blur of fire and shadow. Almost in one motion, he was thrown backward into darkness, swept off his feet, and nearly cut in half.

Now on the jungle floor, reeling from pain, he realized not only something had happened to his eyes, but the explosion had also ripped him wide open, exposing his intestines to rotten jungle stench and dingy bacteria. As he moved his hand down his leg, he felt a huge chunk of metal embedded in his upper right leg, his leg dangling by a few pieces of flesh. Lying helpless on the jungle floor, he heard more incoming rounds. He tried crying out, but it seemed no one heard him above the continuing mortar round explosions. He tried stopping the blood flow by squeezing his flesh, but the pain was too much. He blacked out.

The 173rd mortars rained down on them and did not stop; they pounded his bunker position relentlessly. Finally, the flashes from the rounds gave his comrades a glimpse of his condition—he was bleeding out fast and wouldn't survive without help.

Between the incoming flashes, two soldiers carried the unconscious lieutenant down a winding trail to their underground hospital. They left him and returned to their positions.

When Nghia woke, doctors had stuffed his intestines back in and crudely sutured his stomach, but they were about to amputate his right leg.

He screamed, "No, don't do that! I need my leg! I need my leg!"

They argued with him that they had to amputate, that he would lose it anyway. But Nghia wouldn't give in. He insisted they leave the leg, and after a heated argument, they finally gave in.

"A leg without blood flow will not last long," they told him.

They called for a red-hot metal rod. Orderlies held him down as the doctor pressed the iron into his torn flesh. Nghia's scream tore through the tunnels, then cut off as he slipped back into unconsciousness. When the bleeding stopped, the doctors were confident they'd at least saved his life—if only temporarily.

Moments later, Nghia regained consciousness. This time, he shouted to the doctors, "My pack, my backpack, where's my backpack..." remembering he'd taken it to their well-hidden diversionary camp just before the mortar attack.

"Americans were seen entering the camp, and the packs are all gone," they told him.

The words struck harder than shrapnel. Vu's little book—her gift, her prophecy—was gone. The promise she had spoken over him, that both he and the book would return to her, had been shattered in an instant.

For a moment, even the pain went silent. The tunnels, the voices, the chaos—everything dropped away. Nghia stared into the blackness, gutted, emptied, the prophecy echoing in pieces that no longer fit.

And then, breaking through the silence, came his voice. Raw. Jagged. Torn straight out of the wound. He whispered the poem, each line catching on his breath as if it were the last thing he had left to give:

Remember the date we said good-bye,
I saw tears in your eyes,
and I can't say one word,
even one word of love for you.

You told me to remember to come home to see you.
Six years pass along: no chance to come home.
No chance to see you.
The enemy still there with tanks,
with jets,
with warships.

I must fight.
If I lose, we will see each other next life,
my darling.

PART 3

Looking for a safer way up Hill 1064, one that wouldn't cost more lives, Captain Davis sent several of us on a recon mission. After no more than two hundred and fifty meters of slow, clawing, and crawling through a hot, steamy ocean of green leaves, we accidentally stumbled onto a hidden enemy camp.

We were amazed at the concealment and camouflage used to hide it from intruders, even from the sky above—it was what the PAVN referred to in captured documents as a diversionary camp—in other words, a place they could hide to keep enemy forces off their trail.

I stood near one of its two entrances, scanning the landscape—vertically, horizontally, left to right, up and down. The first thing I noticed at the entrance were stairs leading in and down to the main areas of the camp. Overall, I guesstimated its size to be less than 900 square feet. From the outside, the camp was completely surrounded by thick, green jungle plants of all varieties.

On the inside, we found the camp situated between two mountains that joined at their tops and gradually separated toward one of the entrances. In a quick glance from one side of the camp to the other, I noticed a mountain stream flowing with cool, slow-moving water running through the camp and down the mountain. It curved gently, as if it belonged there, as if it had been cutting this path for years.

I bent over to soak my drive-on rag in the stream, and then, my eyes followed the water's smooth but slight bend—until they landed on a pile of olive-drab rucksacks beside the stream. They were neatly stacked. Prompting a question. "Was their neatness by design, or an accident?"

In another direction, I spotted stair steps leading up one of the mountains on my right, that had been tamped out of black dirt with some sort of tool that packed soft dirt into shape, perfectly measured, that appeared to be as hard as concrete.

That immediately made me curious, so I had to try them out and see if they'd hold my weight. They did. Once back down, a further surprise—I noticed many hammocks tied between the trees, indicating the enemy slept there at night, possibly to avoid getting massacred during a nighttime artillery barrage.

Something in me froze.

They were organized and were actually making the best of jungle life. Better than us, because we had to sleep on the ground, that is, if we got to sleep at all. Somehow, for at least a few seconds, a brain-flash—were these the animals, the targets I'd learned about back on training missions? The ones we dehumanized, the ones that didn't deserve to live. My training taught me to kill anything that carried a weapon. I wasn't trained to hear their voices or see their humanity. But there it was—right in plain view.

The team leader and I noticed the backpacks at the same moment. He grabbed the radio handset from the RTO, or radio telephone operator.

"Alpha Six, Alpha Six, this is Lima Six, come in Alpha Six."

"You got him," Davis replied, "you got a sitrep?" (Situation Report)

"Roger that, Six. We've found a well-camouflaged enemy camp—just a couple of hundred, maybe two-hundred-fifty meters, from our perimeter. We've got backpacks, beaucoup backpacks."

"Backpacks?" Davis shot back. "You got backpacks. How many?"

"Roger that, Six. Looks like about fifty-two. Fifty-two as in Foxtrot Tango."

"All right, listen up," Davis said. "Leave everything else—just grab the packs. Every one of them. Then get out—now."

Back at our perimeter, the backpacks were all dropped in a not-so-neat pile. My platoon sergeant said they all had to be searched. They all looked the same, like they'd been wet and dried many times, similar to ours after only a few months in the super-wet, rain every day jungle we were now in, but as I stood there soaking wet with sweat and burning up from the sun cooking us while looking them over, I got excited on the prospect of seeing and learning first-hand what kinds of things enemies carried.

I grabbed one and sent it to the ground, while Capt. Davis, standing immediately on my left, and LT. Doane, on my right, watched every slow but meticulous move my hands made, unwinding the backpack's green straps from around two brown buttons, used to hold its top flap on tightly.

PAVN Rucksacks discovered on the recon mission conducted by Captain Davis during the Battle of Hill 1064. Scott Murray (front) and Specialist 4 Chapman search contents for information. Paul Reed (not in photo) garnered Lt. Nghia's diary from one of these in the afternoon of March 17, 1968. Photo credit: Wendell "Fritz" Schautz, Alpha Company 1/503d 173d Airborne.

Right under the top flap sat two flags—flashes and images of them hanging on my wall at home quickly dashed through my mind, but Davis quickly said, "Gimme the Viet Cong flag, Reed, gimme that VC flag!" while Doane, apparently interested in a photo opportunity, coerced me out of the other one, and suddenly—the image of them on my wall at home disappeared.

One of two flags Lt. Nghia carried in his rucksack. Platoon leader Lt. John B. Doane displays the flag, Specialist 4 Chapman (far right) holding a photo of Ho Chi Minh. March 17, 1968. Photo credit: Wendell "Fritz" Schautz, Alpha Company 1/503d 173d Airborne.

Continuing my search, I found an almost transparent plastic bag stuffed with several items. Inside, I saw a few photos, military orders, an ID card, and, among other things, a small book, covered in what appeared to be fake alligator skin. It appeared to be a diary. Among the other things inside the bag, I saw what looked like an enemy version of the American Stars and Stripes—a newspaper, but in turning its pages, I couldn't read it, yet I found a name—Ho Chi Minh.

Suddenly, Chapman, who was digging through another one, hollered, "Hey, look at what I got." He was holding a large photo of Ho Chi Minh. I told him I wanted the photo to accompany the newspaper.

"No way," he answered.

Then, immediately, I began focusing on the little book with the fake alligator-skin cover. It measured maybe four inches high, three wide. Outside, it had dried mud on it—caked in the grooves, brittle at the corners—but inside, the pages were clean. White as rice. Untouched.

Outside cover of journal

I thumbed through it slowly, page by page. Tight lines of some of the most beautiful handwriting I'd ever seen. Regardless of the language, this was written with skill—all in Vietnamese. I couldn't read a single word. Not one. But that didn't matter. I knew what I was holding.

Inside of Nguyen Van Nghia's little diary.

It felt like a life, his life. Bound up and still warm. It could've been battle notes. It could have been about the war. It could've been love letters. What it said—or what it didn't wasn't really my concern—but it was his, and I was holding it. And that felt like something. Thrilling, in a way. I didn't want to say anything to Chapman. Maybe that was because I realized it wasn't just a photo or a newspaper—it was something that, if given a chance, could talk.

And this much we knew for certain about the enemy—they had to be strong, hardcore, and invincible. Capturing something like this had weight. It meant something.

Also, I found papers appearing to be military orders. In the lower-left corner, a rubber stamp was printed in red ink, "Twenty-fourth Regiment, 304th PAVN Division." And... about halfway down the page, a name..."Nguyen Van Nghia."

"I hated him, that I know," I wrote in a letter to my parents. "I knew that much about him, and I hated all enemies as I hated him," I said. "He was just somebody I'd learned to hate and kill, only a target."

I saw the resupply bird coming in and didn't even think. I just bolted and made a full-throttle dash through the grass and the heat. I wasn't after food, water, gear, or mail. I wasn't trying to get something from the chopper. I was trying to get something on it. In my hands was the C-ration box that I'd stuffed with the enemy's things I'd taken from the backpack the day before—papers I couldn't read, but somehow felt mattered.

Especially the little fake alligator skin-covered book. Maybe just a feeling, but deep down, I knew that what I'd found was important. Don't ask me how, maybe a hunch, like it was the little book's destiny to fall into enemy hands—mine.

I was the only one running. Everyone else stayed back. I didn't even think about the danger—just had to get to the bird before it lifted off—but failed. Fortunately, right as it started to ascend, the Crew Chief spotted me running toward him, and the bird came back down to a hover. It was then he leaned out, grabbed the box straight from my hands, and pulled it inside.

We couldn't hear each other over the engine noise, but he read my lips when I shrugged and mouthed, I don't have any money to pay for shipping. Letters were free, but boxes cost. He caught it right away, and if I read his lips correctly, he seemed to be saying, "Don't worry, I'll take care of it." Then the bird lifted off and disappeared.

And right then, I felt the greatest relief. Because deep down, I didn't think I was going to live much longer. The fighting had been bad—really bad—and the enemy was bringing in reinforcements daily via the Ho Chi Minh trail. They were coming at us from every direction.

But that box? That box was going home. Somehow, some way, I knew it would make it out. Maybe through destiny, the power that determines the course of events. A part of me would make it out, too.

Walking back to my platoon, I started to doubt, thinking about all the ways that box might never reach my parents. We were in Vietnam. In a war. In the middle of the jungle. The mail got lost. Boxes fell into rice paddies. Choppers got shot down, and door gunners didn't always come through.

However, I confided in at least one thing, the box was in other hands.

PART 4

Tactically, the enemy had placed PAVN snipers well forward of their bunkers to alert their unit of approaching enemies, which was us.

As Alpha Company advanced, sometimes slowing to a crawl because of green, what we called wait-a-minute vines, snagging on almost every piece of equipment on our backs or what we were carrying, toward the summit of Hill 1064, we must have appeared like a string of ants crawling up a massive mountain.

The snipers were located at least a hundred meters to the front of their elaborate fortress, dug into the main ridgeline—Hill 1064. They had a clear view of the valley from the direction we were coming and could pick off just about anyone trying to make it to the summit.

Our point man and the one behind him, a few meters back, came into the sniper's view through the thick vegetation. The enemy opened fire with AKs—killing James G. Blackshear and Patrick J. Tremblay.

James G. Blackshear & Patrick J. Tremblay

Trenches spiraled down the slopes through thick jungle and towering trees. Dense triple-canopy jungle shielded the enemy from artillery, airstrikes, and being overrun. The vegetation made them nearly invisible—both from the air and from Alpha Company below. Any unit—no matter which army—would face a brutal uphill climb from the valley and be physically drained by the time they reached the summit. And beyond sheer exhaustion, the heat and humidity would be suffocating.

The sound of enemy mortars was terrifying—but the waiting was worse. That agonizing fifteen to twenty seconds between launch and impact was more frightening than death itself. Not knowing where it would hit. Not knowing what or who it would rip open. And not knowing if you were going to live or die the moment it landed—those things alone were fearful enough.

Alpha Company lost two good men. With enemy fire pinning everyone down—and snipers making it impossible to recover their bodies—Captain Davis gave the order to pull back and set up a night defensive perimeter (NDP), farther down the hill, closer to the valley.

Paul Reed, humping the eighty-one-millimeter mortar tube to our new perimeter during the Battle for Hill 1064. March 1968.

After hustling to a new mountaintop on Davis's command and hastily digging in, we realized some of the enemy had followed us to our new location. Our first clue was a single sniper round—Daniel Burr had taken a round and thrashed beside a huge rock like a fish out of water.

The sniper's round tore through Daniel's chest and exited his back, leaving two gaping holes. He couldn't breathe through his nose or mouth—air was now escaping through the open bullet wounds. Medics, desperately trying to patch both holes with plastic that protected radio batteries from rain and moisture, said the wounds were called "sucking chest wounds" and that he needed surgery immediately.

Captain Davis requested medevac immediately.

As the medevac chopper began feathering down, enemy fire struck one of the pilots in the foot, forcing me to wave the bird off. Three more times the bird attempted to land, and three more times it was waved off. Wounded, the pilots refused to quit—defying orders, trying again and again to land and get Daniel to surgery before time ran out.

Before I heard the chopper blades of the inbound medevac, I'd low-crawled over to him, intending to try giving him comfort—and this while dodging bullets cracking overhead and pitching grenades down the side of the hill. But he didn't want any sympathy or comfort. He said he was the lucky one getting out of this hellhole, and the rest of us were the unlucky ones. I never responded, as I could see his condition worsening, but he continued, "I'm the lucky one by taking the million-dollar wound, and I'm glad I've done it because I'm headed home. Don't feel sorry for me," he said.

Then suddenly, enemy fire let up long enough for the medevac to land. As soon as it landed, Michael Vigil, Scott Smith, Jerry Thomas, and I, along with one or two others, hustled him onto the bird—and he was gone.

I was happy for him—he was getting out of the hellhole. But that feeling didn't last.

A few minutes later, Davis got a call from the medevac pilot. Burr had expired. It was clear that Daniel thought he was going home. It just wasn't the home he had in mind.

Sgt. Daniel L. Burr, died during the Battle of Hill 1064: March17th, 1968. Alpha Company1/503d 173rd Airborne.

PART 5

One afternoon, the PAVN company commander came above ground to inspect the bunker complex overlooking the valley to the west. His office entrance was a narrow hole dug close to the trunk of a towering tree, wedged tightly between two of its massive roots. The roots climbed nearly five meters up the tree's trunk, anchoring the giant, towering hardwood with quiet strength.

As the commander pulled himself from the small entrance, he noticed Lieutenant Nguyen Van Nghia, a soldier from Thai Binh, flipping through the pages of a small book, the little volume his wife Vu had given him. Normally, that wouldn't have drawn attention—but Nghia's frustration was starting to show, and it piqued the commander's curiosity. When Nghia saw him approaching, he quickly jumped to his feet.

"At ease," the commander said, returning the salute. "I couldn't help but notice how focused you are on that little book, its presence steady, as though it waited to be opened when the time was right," he added, gesturing toward the book.

The commander, a northerner himself, knew it was common for soldiers to keep diaries—often reflections of their inner lives. That only deepened his interest.

"No, sir," Nghia replied quickly. "I'm not writing about the military. Well... not too much, only sometimes. Mostly, I write about my wife, my family, and the life we shared before the war. I was trying to find a particular poem, but I can't remember the page."

"Mostly poetry?" the commander asked.

"Yes, sir." Before he could say more, Nghia added, "I reread it often to keep from feeling lonely."

"You're right," the commander said. "Out here, we all need something to remind us of home. May I take a look?"

"Of course," Nghia said, handing him the book.

The pages were hand-sewn. The cover appeared to be alligator skin—unusual. Flipping through it, the commander noticed the paper was rag, not rice. After a quiet moment of studying the pages, he handed the book back.

"I haven't seen one like this before," he said.

"I'm proud of it," Nghia said. "Most have plain rice paper and glue bindings. But this one... stitched by hand. Would you like to hear how it came to me, sir?"

"I would."

Nghia began. "Well, back in Tai Giang village, in Tien Hai District, my wife bought it from a small store near our home. When we heard the loudspeakers calling for men to go south to fight the American invaders, she and I talked it over for a long time. As a family man, I hesitated, but she and I both eventually agreed that going south to fight was my calling. Said the nation needed me. I must go.

"That night she hosted a going-away dinner. As we sat beside the table, she took my hands in hers and said something I'll never forget, 'Husband, your job as a soldier will be dangerous and filled with hardship. But there is a way your wife can always be with you.'"

The commander's voice softened. "Is that right?" he asked, watching Nghia with a mix of curiosity and quiet respect.

"Yes, sir. She knew I loved writing poetry, a skill I began developing as early as hammer school. When she gave me this book," Nghia said, holding it with both hands and meeting the commander's gaze, "She told me, 'When you fill its pages with poems about your wife, I'll be right there beside you each time you read them.' So that's what I've done. As we moved through the Truong Son mountains, I filled its pages with poems and memories—about her, my family, and our country. She believes both of us will return to her."

"Both of you?" the commander asked.

"Yes," Nghia said. "She told me she had a dream—that I, and this little book, would both return to her. That belief comes from her ancestors. It's part of what was passed down to her."

The commander, reflecting on his own lineage, asked, "And what do you believe?"

"Sir, we lost thousands of men just a few kilometers from here in Dak To. That battle taught us how brutal the Americans can be. We've all heard the stories—how they'll kill us, cut out our livers and hearts, even eat them. They're barbarians. Survival won't be easy, maybe not possible. And we're here until the war is over.

"Based on what happened at Dak To, I think we're in the path of destruction. If not death by gunfire, artillery, then starvation, disease, or snakebite will get us. Food supplies are almost gone. Other than tree roots that taste terrible, our only hope is finding canned food the Americans leave behind in the pits they dug."

"Will I survive?" he asked, holding the commander's gaze. "Will both of us return to her? Ahhh...if only I could believe that. But if she's by my side when my time comes, then I won't be alone. That's what matters most."

The commander said nothing. He understood war—its loss, its cruelty, and the dreams it quietly kills. He didn't want to challenge Nghia's belief, but doubt pressed against the back of his throat. In the end, he let the silence speak for him.

"Did you compose the poems yourself?" he asked instead.

"No, not all," Nghia said. "But the ones about my wife, my family, and my homeland—those are mine. Some poems remind me why I'm a soldier. Others speak about the importance of this fight. And some are for the hardest days—when the urge to give up feels stronger than the will to go on."

"And did you give her something in return?" the commander asked. "A gift from you?"

"Certainly," Nghia replied. "I served in our military during the French occupation, before returning home. And I've lived long enough to know proper etiquette. I carved a flute for her from a short piece of bamboo. I told her that whenever she played it, she'd have me by her side—at least in her mind, that is. She's musically inclined—learned it immediately. Now, when I close my eyes, my mind's eye sees her sitting on our patio, playing."

The commander nodded, slowly and deliberately—more in reverence than agreement, as if weighing the weight of the memory Nghia had just handed him.

"When our young soldiers get homesick," Nghia said, "I hope that hearing memories from an older soldier helps remind them what they're fighting for. When this war is over, and the two heartbeats of this divided country finally beat as one, then I'll be reunited with my wife."

"Ah-ha," the commander said, his tone light but his eyes saying something else. "So, after all, you do believe you'll make it home."

After a moment of silence, Nghia smiled and said, "It's her belief, sir. But after so many years together, I've learned not to argue with her."

Nghia understood the war might be over soon—or it might take much longer. Whatever the outcome, however long it took to drive the Americans out, he was committed. That was the agreement a northern soldier accepted—he would not return home until the war was over—unless he was dead or no longer fit for duty. His wife understood that. She had agreed to wait for him, no matter how long it took. She didn't expect him to die, but was prepared for the possibility, or at least prepared for a long separation.

Lieutenant Nghia was the party officer of his unit, but many times his role felt more like that of an uncle, someone the younger soldiers looked up to and trusted. Though he still fought alongside them, he could relate to the men on a different level. At thirty-nine, he had walked the path they were just beginning. He planned to share the poems he'd written along the Truong Son mountain range with the younger soldiers.

Late one night, a young soldier approached him with a quiet request. He asked Uncle Nghia, using his social title rather than his military rank, if he wouldn't mind reading one of his poems aloud to his fellow soldiers—something to help them sleep.

Without hesitation, Nghia went to them and flipped to a page he had marked. He cleared his throat and read softly:

A LULLABY

Days, then months pass;
A year is twelve months, each with thirty days.
You sit, numbering the days.
Fully six years have passed since I left.
That day your rosy cheeks were flush with youth.
Their brightness still warms me.
The good old days lapsed into
Ongoing struggle.
At home, you still try to stay busy.
Autumn leaves have fallen six times since I left.
You lean against the door, facing the river, hoping.
You lift your gaze to the rosy clouds overhead.
You look around the yard, hoping
But still, see nothing.
The day I left, I promised
That I would return.
I will keep my promise.
You've lost yourself in tending the rice fields
Since the day I left 'til now.
At home, you are still daily hoping;
Your love is like pink silk.
How can I write all that I think of you?

You are a bird, feathered in lotus petals.
What could be brighter than the glow of us together?
The greatest love is yours.
As I lean against this light pole during midwatch,
I gaze at your picture and return your smile;
So sweet is your expression.
Our love is like the sunrise
Shedding light through rosy clouds.
Missing me, you think up some verse;
With this pen, I will jot it down.
I am awkward; I don't know what to say.
How will I finish this letter,
My heart is bursting.
Though far apart,
The distance does not separate us.
We remain joined
In the spring of our lives.

"Oh, wait a minute, did you hear that?" asked Nghia.

"Hear what?" the young soldiers replied.

After a moment or two of silence, Nghia said, "I can hear her playing her flute right this moment. She's playing my favorite tune. It is music to my ears. It's beautiful."

After the faraway look on Nghia's face morphed into a smile, the young soldiers heard him say, "Her music is what keeps me alive. Now think of your own memories and jot them down before it's too late."

As the young soldiers rose to leave, they were reminded of the pact they made earlier. The officer was dead serious—not if, but when the war took his life, the little book was to make its way back to his wife in the north.

"It doesn't matter which of you takes it to her," he said, "but one of you must."

He closed the book. There was no applause, no sound at all, only a stillness that seemed to settle into the very soil. One by one, the younger soldiers lay their heads down, their thoughts drifting far from war.

Nghia didn't expect to survive. But if he did, he would bring the book home. If not, maybe someone else would. Perhaps one of the young soldiers he'd just made a pact with would make sure it found its way back to her, even if he didn't.

Much later that night, the sound of mortar fire echoed through the hills. Nghia's mortar team estimated the firing was approximately five to six hundred meters away from their position, clearly not directed toward them or their bunker complex. And everyone agreed—it was the 173rd they had been warned about.

CHAPTER SIX

FIRE MISSION

Our perimeter was probed from multiple directions, but never breached. Claymores, M-16s and M-60's spit walls of hot led and shrapnel. One enemy we barely saw was mysterously dragged off in the darkness—but how many more lay out there in the thick jungle, watching… waiting… we didn't know.

We fought like cornered animals. Every ounce of strength. Every round in the magazine. Every breath spent in chaos. Brass casings carpeted the ground around our fighting positions. The smell of burnt powder hung thick in the air. No one said it—but we all felt it—death was close. Maybe waiting for one of us before first light.

After the firing died down, Captain Davis approached the hastily dug 81mm mortar pit and gave us a fire mission. The sun had been down for some time when we began preparing. In total darkness, we worked by feel—attaching fuses, setting them by touch on more than thirty 81mm rounds. Each one timed for detonation on impact. We didn't know who was on the receiving end of those rounds—didn't care, and didn't want to.

But this we knew: if Specialist Four Norman Belmore, our FDC, got his math right… and if John Burkhart, our gunner, set the sight correctly… whoever was on top of that summit would soon be dead.

Davis leaned in close and said quietly, "Put the rounds directly on top of the enemy." Then, almost in a whisper, he added, "S-2 indicated during the briefing—it's the 304th Division out of North Vietnam. This surprise should make them wish they were home instead of here."

Belmore, thinking of Jimmy Blackshear and Tremblay—killed earlier that day—checked the coordinates on his plotting board one final time. Then he looked up and said to Burkhart, "Everything's correct." When I heard that, I grabbed a round, eased it halfway into the tube, and said, "Round hangin', sir."

All that stood between that moment and killing the enemy… was one word. I waited.

"Fire!"

I released the round. It dropped, struck the firing pin, and exited the tube with an ear-splitting *boom* that echoed across the valley. Davis stood in the pit. He heard the round leave the tube. Still, Burkhart called out, "Round on the way, sir."

Seconds later, Davis said he saw the explosion—short. About twenty-five meters. "Add twenty-five," he ordered. Belmore made the correction and called out the new data. Burkhart adjusted the sight.

I hung another round…and waited for the command.

Paul Reed (assistant gunner), hanging an eighty-one-millimeter mortar round, about to drop it down the tube and fire during the Battle for Hill 1064. March 1968. John Burkhart (gunner), in the pit holding his ears, lower center.

The 14-pound round shot from the tube with another thunderous boom, echoed throughout the valley like the first. We knew the enemy couldn't help but hear our tube. This time it landed dead center—squarely atop the enemy bunkers crowning Hill 1064.

Before the first round even landed, I'd already launched two or three more HEs (high-explosive rounds) toward 1064. The last round set their powder to cooking, which we called a "secondary." Hitting a secondary doesn't happen more than once in a thousand—but we got lucky. One great blast, then a chain of smaller ones—mortar rounds, maybe grenades, God only knows what—but this I knew, whoever was alive up there was bleeding, mangled by shrapnel, burning, or dead.

That was every mortar crew's hope—to catch a cache. It'd take out anyone nearby and gut their supply of ammo, cutting their ability to return fire. We fired off another fifteen rounds before Davis finally ended the fire mission.

As the sun threatened to rise, Alpha Company prepped for its final assault on Hill 1064. Weapons were checked and rechecked. Magazines were topped off. Grenades were counted. Knives were strapped down. There was no chatter—only the silent understanding that this could be our last day alive.

About halfway up the summit, we hit resistance—AKs, SKSs, and a RPG—but nothing like the day before. Still, Davis wasn't about to get more of his men killed. Somewhere nearby, Davis knew there were jet planes with napalm.

"Gimme that handset," Davis told his battalion RTO, Wendell "Fritz" Schautz, who stayed as close to him as a tight suit.

For a few seconds, Davis fumbled with his list of pushes—radio frequencies—trying to get the right one on the two PRC-25 dials. His hands shook with frustration as movement and enemy chatter grew louder from the ridge above. He swore under his breath while his eyes locked on the summit, determined to make contact for close-air support before Alpha Company made their final charge on Hill 1064.

Finally, Fritz, who was lying beside him in the prone position, had managed to contact an Air Force FDC.

When Fritz got them on the horn, he handed the handset to Davis. He didn't waste a second—barking into the radio, he was clear and forceful. "No strafing. No Vulcans. No mini-guns." Then, louder and sharper, he read off the coordinates with absolute precision. "I want napalm," he said.

The FDC repeated it back to confirm, then told him the birds would be overhead in seconds.

As the FAC—or Forward Air Controller—circled overhead, the pilot radioed Davis to pop smoke. Seconds later, green smoke floated upward, marking Alpha Company's forward position. FAC reported the smoke color to be green.

Behind the smoke and through the haze, all ninety plus of us in Alpha Company, only a few feet from one another, fanned out along the slope, each man hunched forward, M-16 tight in his grip, eyes locked on the rim of Hill 1064.

We pressed our faces onto the earth, holding on as if it could save us. But the jets—only a hundred meters or so above—tore the sky apart, and even the ground we trusted trembled. After circling once or twice, the first jet came in at treetop level and let go of two cigar-looking canisters that plummeted end over end toward the enemy, hitting a little shy of the target. In the distance, another lined up and, coming in directly above us, dropped two canisters—making it a one-two punch on the hilltop.

In an instant, the entire hillside in front of us went up in flames. The summit had gone dead quiet—no voices, no AK bursts, no whistling RPGs, grenades, or mortars. The napalm had done its job. Flames still licked the tree line as we moved up, stunned to find a clear path and—against all odds—we had no casualties.

Once inside the enemy position, the scene came into focus: several shallow graves bulging with bodies, collapsed bunkers, as many as eight to ten enemy dead scattered across the hill—some burned, others torn apart—even a tail fin or two from the mortars we fired the night before. It was a foul mix—scorched jungle and the unmistakable stench of death, with the taste of charred flesh clinging to every breath.

Before breaching the summit, Alpha Company recovered the bodies of Blackshear and Tremblay. It had only been two days—but in that heat, it felt like weeks. They lay face down where they had fallen—burned, swollen… barely recognizable as men. I used to get letters from Jimmy's grandmother, Flo Cady, down in Florida. Gentle letters. Encouraging. A touch of home in a place that had none.

Later, she wrote to me—said she'd been told he was killed. She never knew how. I made sure she never would.

When we rolled them over, the jungle had already begun its work. Their eyes were gone. The sockets alive—moving—with white maggots. The smell hit first… thick, rotten… something that didn't belong in the world of the living. Something that doesn't leave a man once it finds him. When we tried to lift them, the flesh slipped loose from the bone—like overcooked meat. Hands pulling back. Skin giving way. We weren't zipping body bags. We were gathering what was left of our friends.

That's when I vomited. Not from weakness. From understanding.

This… is what waited for us.

And it could be me tomorrow.

Soon after Kontum, Alpha Company, 1st Battalion, 503rd Infantry, was moved east into Bình Định Province near the South China Sea. I had eleven months left in country.

Eleven more months in this hellhole.

I knew Bình Định. I'd been to the 173rd Airborne Brigade base camp located on Highway 19 before going to Pleiku, on my way to Kontum. There, I learned about the mountain passes along the highway, An Khe and Minh Yang, from troopers who had first-hand knowledge. I hadn't bled there yet, but this I knew:

The jungle wasn't finished with me. There would be more hills, more fire missions, and more wounded dragged downhill and uphill. More nights listening for movement in the dark.

Eleven months more of the heat and humidity so thick it pressed on your lungs.

Eleven more months of punji pits, malaria, and men with rifles who wanted you dead, along with every blood-sucking leech and poisonous snake the jungle had to offer.

Eleven more months of no electricity, no showers, no clean sheets, no relief, nothing but the prospect of dying and trying not to end up in a body bag like Blackshear and Tremblay.

During training, Sarge used to say, "There are only two kinds of people in this world—the quick and the dead." It turned out he wasn't wrong. Staying alive wasn't a science. It was instinct, speed, and whatever skills you could learn fast enough, because slow learners didn't last.

In a letter home, I told my parents not to worry. I wrote that if I died, God wouldn't send me to Hell. I'd already been there. I was living in it.

I still told myself I'd make it out. But after the last twenty days, home felt less like a destination and more like something I once believed in. What mattered most wasn't sleep. Not comfort. Not even survival.

It was that the fake alligator-skin book had already made it home—to my parents.

Ahead of me.

Waiting.

CHAPTER SEVEN

HIS PAPERS

At a field hospital not far from Cherry Hill, Nghia still suffered from his wounds when doctors said they had done all they could.

"Your wounds might still be raw, but you have to go," they said while preparing for him to leave.

They helped him climb out of the crude underground hospital, into the thick green jungle above. No signs. No maps. No directions. Just the jungle. The doctors knew he might collapse and die without assistance. But there was nothing more they could do.

Though his heart still beat, his wounds were worse than those who'd already died. Malaria, dampness underground, and infection made healing impossible. He remembered the night his fellow soldiers carried him underground—the battle was still burning, and the doctors were doubting he would survive. He vowed to return and fight.

He was forced to leave because he had reached the third status of a PAVN soldier at war. He knew the rules. No soldier went home except for one of three reasons:

No. 1 The war was over.
No. 2 The soldier was dead.
No. 3 The soldier was as good as dead and totally useless.

Nguyen Van Nghia was now useless to the war effort—alive, but discarded. He never really thought about dying in the hospital. He just never knew what had kept him alive, or for what reason. Still, he believed if he did recover, he'd return to war.

He could stand, barely. He hobbled, favoring the leg he almost lost, toward where he thought his unit's bunker complex had been atop Cherry Hill—Hill 1064 to the Americans.

He assumed that the Americans would be seen in every direction and that he had to be mindful not only of ground forces, but also of helicopters and jets with rockets and bombs. But as he surveyed his surroundings with his one good eye and two good ears, all he heard were the familiar sounds of the jungle.

American bombs had turned it to dust. The foxholes and bunkers he built with his men—gone. Trees above the tunnels were blasted to splinters—giant toothpicks still smoldering like the end of a cigarette.

His foremost thought, beyond the eerie silence, was that no one was there to greet him. No sentry. No defender. No countrymen. They were all gone.

He remembered the night a mortar round almost split him in half. Now, he saw what was left—no unit, no hope. Just a broken body and worse morale.

He was totally alone. In all of his forty years he'd never felt as alone as he was at this moment.

Before the Americans attacked, he remembered peering through thick green vegetation. Now there was nothing. No trees. No foliage. No camouflage. He knew if the enemy flew over, he could be seen easily.

And worse, all his buddies had died. The smell—it was the stench of death. He staggered to the shallow graves holding the rotting corpses of soldiers he once knew from the Truong Son trail. Jungle heat, maggots, insects, and dampness had begun absorbing them into the earth. But their images were burned into his mind.

He stood and saluted, whispering a vow—they would never be forgotten. Then his physical wounds became secondary. They didn't matter.

While scanning for enemy movement, trying to guess what direction to go, he spotted where their diversionary camp had been. A horrendous thought hit him—the Americans had overrun it. He remembered the dream his wife had told him—that he and the little book would find their way back to her. She had vowed to be at his side always, a vow he touched again and again when he read the poems he had written in her name.

There was just one problem. His backpack containing the small book was gone forever. It was a thought that hit harder than shrapnel—worse than when his belly was torn open by an American mortar round.

That little notebook had gone everywhere with him—almost as if it were destiny—pocket, backpack, the whole trek south. He carried it like it was worth more than fine gold, its words reaching where no bullet could ever reach. Losing it felt like losing her. As if she had died.

The wounds didn't matter anymore. What cut deepest was knowing she was lost to him forever—never again at his side. He thought of the pact he made with the young soldiers. Knowing the little book would never one day make it home was like a broken promise. That alone brought him to his knees, his hands covering his face.

But then, just as he sank into that thought, he heard her flute. Faintly, as if from another world. It was her. Her flute. The same melody he'd written about. Tears filled his eyes. They were two people with one heart. The poem returned to him, word for word and he calmed. From then on, when despair took hold, he recited what he'd memorized. That was how he'd keep her close.

He waited for sundown, picked a direction, and set out. Night by night, he crept along jungle trails. Hiding by day, moving under the cover of darkness. No food. No water. No medicine. No clean clothes. He used a tree limb as a crutch and kept going.

Eventually, he reached a village. The houses were up on stilts—unlike home. Probably for the monsoon season, he guessed. A villager saw him and offered help. They couldn't speak to each other. Nghia drew maps in the dirt. The villager pointed to Laos.

He'd been going in the wrong direction—nearly a month off course.

The man took him in, gave him food and shelter.

But the next morning, Nghia had a fever—malaria. The villager didn't let him leave. Instead, he nursed him back to health. When Nghia regained his senses weeks later, he was stunned to learn how long he'd been unconscious.

Two weeks after that, he found a military checkpoint. But no one had time for him, and supplies were short. The war still raged in the south. The young and strong were heading south.

Nghia looked old. He was feeble, near blind, and using a crutch. To most, he looked like he'd die before reaching the next bend in the trail. And beyond that bend, the trail was being bombed daily.

He often got lost. Collapsed. Fever returned. Villagers along the way gave what little they could. It was the only thing that kept him alive.

He remembered the slogans: *Fight to the last bullet, last drop of blood. For unification. For independence.* But some days, he thought of giving up.

One day, he stumbled into a dark, bombed-out village. PAVN soldiers lay scattered across the ground. A battle had taken place here—but with whom, he didn't know. He moved through the wreckage slowly, stepping past the dead. No voices. No movement. Only the stillness that follows violence. One of the bodies had a pistol. Nghia knelt, took it, and stood. He walked to a blackened burn pit and stopped. For a long moment, he just stood there...

staring into it. Then he raised the pistol and pressed it against his head. He pulled the trigger. The hammer fell. Nothing.

He lowered the weapon, found a single round, and slid it into the chamber. His hands were steady now. Too steady. He raised the pistol again. His finger tightened on the trigger—and then… he heard it. A flute.

Soft. Distant. Familiar. The same melody. His finger stopped. He listened. Not with his ears alone—but with something deeper. Something that had not been destroyed. The pistol slipped from his hand and hung at his side. His eyes filled. He saw her—Vu—waiting… playing… believing he would return. The weight inside him shifted. Not gone. Not healed. But no longer alone. He lowered the weapon.

And chose to keep going.

Nghia spent many nights hobbling along kilometers and kilometers of jungle trails. He was always hiding, hungry, and listening for tigers, fearful of being eaten. Losing his sight made the journey more difficult. Now he was losing strength.

He could hear Vu play her flute, which kept him from losing hope. Getting home to her was the only thing that mattered.

After nearly two years of wandering north with relapses of malaria and fever, hungry and blind, stumbling and falling, he spotted his own backyard.

Vu saw him first. She didn't recognize him. He was bent over. Limping with a homemade crutch. A shadow of the man she once knew.

She remembered the day the military told her he was dead two years earlier. But through all the years, something kept pulling at her.

He saw her.

She didn't move.

Doesn't she know who I am? he thought.

She whispered, "No... that can't be Nghia. He was strong. Proud. This bent old man couldn't be him."

But it was him. As he reached the patio, she touched him. He was not a ghost as she had imagined, but real.

He was wrecked. Barely on his feet. But he found the strength to say, "Your flute. Your flute. I heard you playing."

Before they sank to their knees in a newlywed's embrace, she spoke, "The Army told me back in March 1968 that you had died in Kontum."

But now her heart soared—he wasn't some shadow or ghost of the man she loved. He was here, real, in her arms. He shared his thoughts, and she learned about his poetry and writings. How he had held on to words deep in his heart where no bullet could ever reach. How the Americans had taken his book, which was now gone forever.

He needed help, so she took him to the doctor.

"He's got to prove his identity. No ID, no treatment," the doctor shouted, slamming the door in her face.

"That's impossible!" she screamed. "The Americans got his papers—they're gone forever!"

CHAPTER EIGHT

WOUNDS I CARRIED

Back home, I lost the underground, earth-covered, solid-concrete house my father and I had built. It had been more than a roof over my head—it was the life my father helped me carve out in the side of a hill. Side by side, we built a refuge to stand against almost any kind of battle, especially Texas tornadoes, helping to turn battle scars into shelter.

Eventually, I realized it was a bunker in all but name. One way in, one way out. It echoed the strongholds of war, but this one was for my family—lots of protection.

The inevitable happened one night when the lines between my wife and me crossed. Words were said, things were thrown, it was the kind of night that makes the walls feel like they're closing in. That's the night the sheriff looked me in the eye and said, "You need to leave—for now. It'll be better this way."

So, I walked out of the house that was part of my soul, away from my son, and into a fog I didn't yet recognize—PTSD. At the time, it felt like a matter of survival. I thought, *Just get out. Just make it through the night.*

But leaving was never simple. It meant the slow tearing apart of everything I spent part of my life building—the house where my son, Silas, had taken his first steps, the only home he'd ever known. I left because I thought it would de-escalate things. I thought it would show I wasn't the problem. I thought it was temporary.

But leaving that house didn't just mean giving her space—it meant giving up ground. Legal ground. Emotional ground. The sheriff didn't say that part.

And once I was out, everything else started slipping away.

That house... it wasn't just a roof. I'd poured everything into it—money, sweat, dreams. Losing it to the mortgage company felt like watching a piece of myself get bulldozed. Like I'd been stripped of my worth as a man, a father. Like nothing I did mattered anymore. And later, I learned no judge in the world would give custody of a boy to a man who had no home—yes, I was homeless.

I started living under an overpass outside town. Cardboard and diesel fumes. Nightmares at 2 a.m. felt more real than the life I was waking up to. I'd been out of Vietnam just a short while, but the war wasn't over—not inside me. I was still in it. Still jumping at shadows, sounds, smells, and still living the accepted belief that I was worth something.

Every time I saw a child with their parents, I thought of Silas. And every time I looked at the hard concrete above me and the empty space around me, I somehow knew I was to be a man and to overcome. For him.

I dreamed of finding a trucking job. For the pay. For the one sliver of stability it could provide. I made myself believe I could rebuild from there, that one day I'd walk into that courtroom with a real address. That I could look the judge in the eye and say, "I've got a roof. I've got a job. I've got a home for my boy."

But deep down, I was still breaking. PTSD doesn't go away just because you find a place to sleep. It follows you, invades your mind, poisons your friendships, your marriage, sits next to you at dinner, rides with you in the cab of the truck, whispers in your ear at red lights—and most of the time, you don't see it coming.

Long before I was sleeping under bridges, I'd learned what it felt like to live inside a choke point. Highway 19 in Vietnam was one of them.

And after Kontum, Alpha Company was shifted east into Bình Định Province, operating out of Camp Radcliff at An Khê. The road that mattered most was Highway 19—the narrow ribbon that ran from the coast, climbed through the An Khê Pass, and cut its way into the highlands. Every convoy, every supply run, every movement in or out of the Central Highlands depended on that road. And the enemy knew it.

Fire Support Base Schuller sat below a bend in Highway 19, from which my platoon, *Oscar Platoon*, was assigned to guard at both ends of Bridge 24. From our vantage point, slightly higher than Schuller's, we could see the lifeline of the war threading through the jungle and the mountain. It was beautiful from a distance. Up close, it was a kill zone—Schuller got mortared almost every day—and we watched, unable to help or do anything, Americans colliding with exploding enemy mortar fire, killing them instantly.

The Operations Report—*Lessons Learned* document in early 1968 confirmed that A-1-503d was involved in an action on Highway 19:

> *An NVA force from the 95th B NVA Regiment attempted to ambush an American convoy along Highway 19 between the An Khê Pass and the Mang Yang Pass. The ambush failed. A-1-503d had been called in to repel the ambush. A short time later, forty-six deceased enemy lay scattered all over the terrain. Four were captured.*

That's how history writes it.

What it doesn't say is what it feels like to stand there afterward—boots in red dirt, rifle hanging from your shoulder, watching a bulldozer carve a trench in the earth while close to fifty men, who were still breathing hours earlier, had to be gathered and lowered into a mass grave, their war ending in silence and soil.

Captain Davis informed me that the mass grave the bulldozer driver dug, beside the road they had tried to claim, was the same stretch of ground on Highway 19—near Mang Yang pass—where, years earlier in July 1954, the Battle of Mang Yang Pass, also known as the Battle of An Khe, occurred. Nearly 1,000 French men lost their lives or were captured in another war, under another flag, on the same cursed earth. Their remains were transferred to France in 1886-87.

Different uniforms. Same ending.

I didn't think about that then. I didn't have the luxury.

But years later, sitting in a truck cab in Wyoming, Idaho, or Montana, watching traffic creep through mountain passes, I would feel it rise in me, that tightening in my chest, my scanning eyes, the sense that every bend in the road was an ambush waiting to happen.

Highway 19 followed me home. It lived on my shoulders, in my sleep, and in the way I read every room before sitting down. In the way I measured exits, angles, and people's hands.

The record backs up what my body already knew. I had learned how to survive in places where men were fed into history in piles. And I never learned how to stop.

I told myself, " You need to hold it together. You've already lost too much. You can't lose your son, too.

The day the mortgage company claimed the house and the land, it was as if they had ripped my life apart, piece by piece. I watched the memories all unravel in slow motion: the earth-covered structure built with my father, the soil I sweated over, the ground I poured my heart over. My father tried to save it, offering partial payments. But they said no and turned us away. It was then that I realized the truth—there was no saving it.

Thoughts on ending it all came up.

Not in a cry-for-help way, either. Just... a quiet exit. Make it stop. I knew where I could go. I knew what to do. The idea carried weight, like a steel anchor in my chest.

But then something cracked through the darkness.

I saw my son, Silas. Not in front of me—just in a vision. His face. The look he'd have if I disappeared. And that was enough.

I couldn't do that to him.

So, I kept going.

That's when Bill McAnally gave me some hope by offering a driving job. His proposal was driving a Freightliner with a V-12 Detroit diesel—hauling chickens coast to coast for a wildcat outfit. Miami to L.A., back and forth, dodging weigh stations with no legal authority to be on the road. Every run would be a risk. Jail time if caught. I didn't care.

The job came with a bunkhouse halfway between loads at the truck yard. A dirty shanty that was never cleaned. Since there was no plumbing, there was no running water or shower. McAnally looked at me and said, "Real men need those things on the road."

I slept there between hauls, trying to outrun everything falling apart behind me. I no longer had a home. Now all I had was a semi-truck, the road, and whatever was waiting at the end of the next trip.

I was burning through fuel and time, but going nowhere. What little money I made disappeared. Some weeks, there was nothing to eat but black beans and stale bread. For days, I sat in a parking lot in Miami waiting for a load that never came, angry and hollowed out.

Miami, that's where I first felt that moment when everything started to slip. I hadn't seen my son, Silas, in weeks. I was broke. Exhausted. Alone.

Several days later, my dad found me in that filthy bunkhouse. "Your mother and I talked it over," he said. "Come home. Take your old room. It's yours until you can get back on your feet."

I resisted. Told him I was a grown man.

But he just looked at me and said, "You have to."

I barked back, "What did you say?"

He snapped, "No court is going to give your son to a man with no home."

He was right, so I moved in with my parents.

I filed motion after motion to get custody of Silas. But the judge wouldn't budge. Said he'd spoken to the boy. Saw no harm. But I knew better. I saw what was happening. I could feel it.

Then the call came, there was a serious accident. The report told the rest: They smelled alcohol on her breath and found drugs in the glovebox. They took a man who had been riding in the car to jail.

Before the judge, the Highway Patrol officer who investigated the 2 am single-car wreck testified. "We found drugs, including marijuana and a couple of other controlled substances. The man who was thrown from the car during the rollover wreck was suspected of criminal DUI and taken to jail, because there were injuries."

His testimony was the turning point. At our next custody hearing, the judge slammed his hand on the bench and reversed everything, saying, "The boy goes with his father."

I didn't cheer. I didn't smile. Because I hadn't won, I'd just been the last man standing.

After all the nights I spent in a truck bunkhouse or parked under an overpass, wondering if my son was warm and if I'd ever see him again, it all came down to a police report and the testimony of a Texas Highway Patrolman.

The courtroom emptied, but I stayed seated. I kept thinking about what the sheriff told me the night I left, "It'll be better this way."

It didn't feel better. It felt like fallout. Deep down, I knew this was just the beginning—not the end—of what the war had done to me. I'd been home from war for a while, but in so many ways, I was still lost in it.

I picked Silas up from school the next day.

He stood there on the sidewalk, shoulders stiff, backpack hanging too low. When he saw me, he didn't smile. Just looked past me, like I was another adult here to change the rules on him again.

On the drive home, he didn't say much. I tried. Small talk about his teacher, a joke about my old truck driving job. Nothing stuck.

We played catch in the yard. We tried to find some rhythm. But the damage ran deep. For both of us.

That night, after dinner, I tucked him in.

"You're safe now," I told him. "Things are going to be better. I promise."

He nodded—but his eyes told the truth. They looked like mine had, once—back in Kontum. He'd seen too much, and he wasn't sure who to trust anymore. Least of all me.

I wanted to hold him. Tell him everything would be okay. But I couldn't promise that. Not really. Not when my own head was still full of night terrors and flashbacks, of ghosts with rifles and helicopters screaming overhead.

That night, he lay there wide awake, staring at the ceiling. And I sat in the hall, listening to his breathing. Wanting to be the father he needed. Wishing I knew how.

Then one night, I exploded. Silas cried. Told me he missed his mom. Said he'd rather be with her. And I broke. All the weight came down at once. I lashed out, and then it was too late. He didn't understand he'd been rescued from danger. He just knew he'd been taken from one storm into another.

I left the house that night and found a booth at a truck stop. Fought two guys I didn't even know and returned home with two black eyes I couldn't explain.

I tried to hold things together. But the truth was starting to surface—quiet, undeniable. I wasn't just a man down on his luck. I was a soldier who never made it home. Not really.

The war never left me.

The anger.

The nightmares.

The sudden, irrational rage.

The fear I didn't show, but always carried.

The record backs up what my body already knew.

In the jungle, you learned to read shadows, to distrust silence, and you always lived one inch from violence.

The Operations Report—Lessons Learned (formerly classified, now unclassified) was a document that indicated where the contacts occurred. It gave the dates and grid squares.

What it cannot tell you is how your shoulders never drop. How your eyes never stop moving. How your body forgets what peace feels like.

We weren't just fighting the enemy anymore. We were:

- Fighting the waiting.
- Fighting the road.
- Fighting the certainty that something unseen was always about to happen.

That's where the war followed me home. It had only been a few years since leaving Vietnam, but that's not enough time. Not with the kind of wounds I was carrying.

CHAPTER NINE

BACK IN THE NORTH

Vu Thi Gai was visibly upset. Her husband needed medical care, but the doctors denied him. He was a career military man and was due a pension, but the government denied that as well. No one in the province could get those benefits without proper identification.

She found out that the government would not treat him or provide any military pension unless he could prove his family tree, place of birth, year of birth, and present records showing he'd been in the military.

Vu told the People's Committee chairman, "I have nothing, no papers of any kind. They were lost in the war. Surely there is something you can do for him. Can't you see he needs help? He is a weak and wounded man."

She raised his shirt and pointed to the terrible scars across his stomach and leg. His skin sunken and jagged, the way only war leaves its mark.

"Yes, of course, I can see those," he replied while studying the disfiguring scars. "But my hands are tied. We've run into this situation before, and he'll have to prove who he is in court. Those are the rules. Once he's done that, he can get new identification papers and get on with his life. Until then, he'll have to get along the best he knows how, the same as all the other people in the province."

Back at home, Nghia felt frustrated by his wife's failed efforts to get him the care he needed and struggled with the idea of telling her about his war experiences. He didn't really know where to start—so much had happened, so many things he wasn't proud of.

He reasoned that if he told her, she'd at least focus not so much on the doctors and committeemen who were rejecting his request for the things he'd earned but instead on the Americans and the war that caused all this grief. Once she understood, it might calm her resentment towards their government workers.

He explained his struggles during the years he was away as best as he could, starting with his trip south on the Truong Son range, where the little book she'd given him years ago first came into the picture.

His story took her across streams and above tall mountains, forging deep rivers on a journey that always forced them to watch for the enemy's huge guns and huge bombs. There was never enough sleep, enough food, or enough medicine, never enough hours in the day to cover the kilometers their leaders demanded. They were exhausted all hours of the day and night.

And he let her know he wasn't upset with the local doctors or the People's Committee for denying the services and things he'd earned. He'd gone years without those things in the south, so he wanted Vu to understand how fortunate he was to be home, even though weak and seriously wounded.

When he tried to tell her, it felt like the words themselves were knives, tearing up his throat, choking him raw. Head down, Nghia tried to hide the tears, but she pulled his chin up with her index finger and looked him in the eyes.

She told him she loved him deeply, and she was happy he was home again, back with the family. Her warmth, her gentle touch—soothing and caressing—is what he had missed for so many years.

Through her tears, he told her he was grateful she played the little flute he'd given her. "I heard you playing many times." When she perked up and asked, "Really?" he confided it was only his imagination, but in the end, hearing her still got him home.

She knew his papers and the little book she'd given him went missing, but she said it was more important to have him home alive without those things rather than him being dead with them. That was her personality. She was the best companion he could ever hope for, and he reassured her while making her a cup of hot tea as they got ready to retire for the night.

The next morning, after a restful sleep, they were off to see a man and his wife who also had a soldier in the war and wanted to hear a fresh report of how the war in the south was going. The son of their closest friend had joined the army and had gone south to fight, but they hadn't heard anything from him in over five years.

"My wife only heard from me once in five years," Nghia told them as signs of deep sorrow covered their faces.

Vu told them about the little book, about her husband's gift of writing poetry, and how she had given it to him before he left to go south to fight. She told them of her dream about both him and the little book returning to her one day. Amazed that her husband returned as she had dreamt, yet they were curious about the little book, "Has it also returned?" they asked.

Nghia spoke up. "It was lost in the jungle," he said quickly while he sprang up, fleeing toward the door. He had exposed a raw hurt he cared to keep to himself. But as he touched the door, something gripped him. He turned back, his eyes heavy, and said, "I will stay and tell you the details, regardless of the personal cost."

They were anxious to hear because they had not traveled the great distances he had, and they said they were happy he had stayed. After a while of talking, he came to the part about his unit's diversionary camp, the place where they stored backpacks and ammo, used as a retreat to keep the Americans off-balance.

To help them understand the principle behind diversionary camps in battle, he explained cooking without smoke as an example because they all understood eating and cooking. In the jungle, that was very important because helicopters could see white smoke against the green jungle backdrop and easily fire on them.

"Because of the smoke, we cooked underground. We dug tunnels or long vents just beneath the Earth's crust, leading away from where we actually cooked. The underground tunnels carried the smoke to other areas by as much as 100 meters or more."

He didn't say that smoke didn't rise from the trees because it did. But the location where the smoke rose was far from where they cooked. The helicopters fired at the smoke, missing their camp, so they could live yet another day.

But they didn't always have to worry about cooking rice and making smoke, he told them. With a somber expression on his face, he said, "Sometimes there was nothing except tree roots to eat."

About that time, Vu cleared her throat and interrupted. "When you left, dear husband, you were only missing one incisor tooth, but now you are missing the one on the other side."

Nghia had lost the first one on the left during the French war. She knew about that one. What she didn't know was how he lost the other one on the opposite side.

"Oh," he chuckled, "that one got whacked out under the same circumstances. A soldier backed into me on the Truong Son range trail."

Now, he was missing two teeth. One was lost during the French War, and the other during the American War.

After they chuckled a moment, he scratched his head, wondering if they understood the principle behind the cooking without the smoke story, that is, not just the reason, but how it saved lives. Because in the story, he was about to let them in on, the principle was the same—they saved lives by keeping the Americans off-balance.

"We believed, because our diversionary camp was well concealed, the Americans could never in a million years locate the camp. That's why we stored our gear there. All our ammo, hospital supplies, and, of course, our backpacks." His brow tightened, "The Americans were never supposed to find that camp.

Nghia continued, "The diversionary or camouflaged camp, as our commander liked to call it, was between two mountains and extremely difficult to find, especially for those clawing their way through the jungle. It was naturally hidden and nearly impossible for helicopters to see because of tall, thickly bunched-together trees.

Only two to three hundred meters from our main battle positions, the camouflaged camp was easy enough for everyone in the unit to locate. Sometimes there were emergency drills, and we did practice runs between battle positions and the camp. We timed the fastest runners to learn how long evacuation might take if the artillery came.

"Inside, the camp we had many of the comforts of home: a freshwater stream which meant water for drinking and uniform washing, shade from the sun's dreadful heat, plenty of trees for our hammocks, and stair steps leading up one side of the camp's mountainous slope."

One of the people broke in, assuming he'd add a little humor to lighten the story. "That sounds like an oasis of peace in the middle of a war zone," he said, but then realized it wasn't funny after the shared look he got.

"During the battle for Cherry Hill that we occupied, somehow the Americans had gotten into our diversionary camp. Our camp was meant to keep the Americans off-balance. I only found out about the Americans getting into our secret camp while I was in the underground hospital," Nghia said before pausing.

One of the neighbors interrupted, asking, "Why did they call the hill they were on Cherry Hill?"

Nghia cleared his throat and said, “We occupied a hill that was part of a cluster of hills named after an earlier battle. Both blood and cherries are red—the cluster was the location where the blood of thousands and thousands of PAVN soldiers got spilled.”

After a moment of reflection, he got back to the part when doctors were about to amputate his leg. “When I got ripped almost in half by an American mortar, I was dragged to our underground hospital. That’s when the Doctors told me that our backpacks had all been taken by the Americans.”

But when he finished, his chest caved, and the tears came—everything he had, everything that mattered, every reason for the fight was in that backpack. They could see it in his eyes, in the collapse of his voice, something deep inside him had been lost forever.

“The Americans were not supposed to find the camp,” Nghia blurted emotionally, and with a raised voice, “It wasn’t just a dirty old, sweaty backpack containing flags, photos, identification papers, and news articles from Hanoi.” He said, trying to disguise his true sorrow at losing the little book, but the tears falling from his cheeks told a different story.

“Something more painful than death,” a tearful Nghia said, meaning, “When Vu is no longer by my side.” A curious look came over them, like what did he mean?

“My backpack is gone forever,” he said, his voice breaking.

The dream his wife clung to before he went south to fight—the dream that both he and the little book would return—had not fully come true. He had made it back, but not the little book.

Vu knew what had happened and the truth they all lived with—his belongings were gone, stripped by faceless hands, contents rifled, papers scattered, the book discarded or burned. Together, they accepted they would never see the book again.

What Nghia didn’t know—what would have ripped him wide open—was that someone had kept it. That the book had been slipped, almost secretly, into a C-ration box by a man named Paul Reed, shipped across the ocean while Nghia lay rotting with infection and malaria in a stinking, dark, damp underground jungle hospital.

His book had reached America nearly two years before Nghia himself ever staggered home. Had he known that truth, it would have cut deeper than any wound. It would have felt like a private kind of death, silent and merciless.

CHAPTER TEN

CHAT WITH GOD

McAnally called, saying he had a load of chickens for Albuquerque, so I headed to the chicken farm to pick up the load.

The good thing about the job with his trucking company was that I was able to attend my church's Wednesday night prayer service fairly regularly. But because of my time in the military, my personality didn't always mesh with others.

Such was the case with a man named Tony Bagwell. Much of the time, he came off as abrasive, overpowering, and forceful in what he believed about God—and how everyone should believe the same way.

What the heck, I thought. I was out of the military and wanted no part of being told what to believe or how to believe it.

Unfortunately, friction and confrontation developed between Tony and me, and each of us showed discord and dislike, if not outright hatred, for the other. At first, we tried to hide our dislike and disrespect, but eventually others noticed.

We wouldn't even speak on Sundays. If one of us saw the other coming down the aisle, we'd quickly move to the opposite side—anything to avoid a face-to-face moment where we'd be forced to speak.

When it seemed there would be no end to our petty behavior, I found a new church home. But after several months, I returned, and before long, our hatred for each other became common knowledge in town. As God-fearing men, we both knew that kind of behavior wouldn't be accepted—but our pride kept us from making things right.

On the road to Albuquerque, at about 1 a.m., my truck rolled along better than a mile a minute. I was thinking about getting the load off as quickly as possible and heading back home when, suddenly, something unexpected happened; my heart started racing.

And I don't mean a little bit. The pounding got harder and faster, until it felt like it might explode. I'd been tired, sure—but this wasn't just fatigue. This was something else. It made no sense... except that something else was happening.

Joy—of all things—started surging through my entire body. I'd never felt anything like it. Not like this. And right then—out of nowhere, I heard my own voice say something I never thought I'd hear myself say, *I love Tony.*

I would never have said that. Not in a million years. That wasn't me. It had to be God.

But then...I said it again. And again. Each time I said it, the hatred that snared me for Tony melted a little more—until finally, it was gone. What replaced it wasn't just peace—something warm. Deep. Joyful.

I didn't understand what was happening, but I knew I'd just witnessed something real. God had spoken. And He used my own voice to do it.

A friend once told me that God could speak through birds, or wind, or animals. I never really believed that stuff. But I believed it now. Because I heard it and experienced it myself.

Not a voice from the sky—but my voice, saying words I didn't believe...until I did.

In the space of five or six miles, everything changed. I didn't just forgive Tony—I loved him. My heart had changed in a way I never thought possible.

And then came something else. Another message—but this one wasn't out loud. It was internal. Like a clear signal. A transmission I could feel. "Tony and I are friends now. It's done."

Huh? I was dumbfounded. It was one thing to say I loved him—but now God was telling me everything between us was wiped clean? That the slate had been washed? I didn't know how to respond.

So, I asked—out loud, as if someone was in the cab with me, before glancing toward the passenger seat, "What is this all about?"

Another clear message, "When you get home, go to Tony's house. Just walk in like you are family. You have no enemy in Tony. Just walk into his house."

I was shocked, amazed—even skeptical. But I knew I'd do it.

As the miles passed, I thought about all our old arguments. Could we really be friends now? My hands gripped the wheel as I dropped gears and rolled downhill into Albuquerque. I kept my eyes between the lines and tried to make sense of what had just happened.

But I didn't doubt it. God had spoken. And I'd heard it with my own ears—through my own lips. My heart had changed from hate...to love. And that was a miracle.

I asked, "But why? Why now? Why on this stretch of highway? On this night?"

Then came the answer, "Tony won't be around much longer."

The truck cab went quiet. Just engine noise, the wind against the doors, and the wheels humming. Then silence. I'd received the message. And I knew it was serious. It wasn't about Tony leaving town—or going to a new church. It meant Tony would soon be gone from this earth.

I backed my rig into the dock in Albuquerque and set the brakes. Two hours later, McAnally called and said no return load was available. I'd have to deadhead back.

While grabbing lunch at a truck stop just outside town, I figured I could make it back in time for Wednesday night prayer service if I hurried.

The service had already started—I was ten minutes late—when I slipped into the church and sat down. Pastor Terry had already prayed and asked if anyone had a testimony.

Tony Bagwell stepped to the podium.

No one knew what was coming—but, according to the communication from God the night before on the way to Albuquerque, I felt uneasy. Without thinking, I hoped what he had to say wasn't what I'd been warned about.

Tony started talking about family. The importance of family... and life... and love. Then he paused. He'd been to the doctor.

"I have cancer and only six months to live."

He didn't want tears. He didn't want sympathy. He said he was fully in God's hands.

Not long after stepping down from the podium, Tony said he wanted to be baptized.

And at that still moment, I cried out, "I do too."

We were baptized together, and while still dripping wet, we looked at each other in the little room behind the baptistery.

Tony said, "I want your forgiveness."

I said, "I already gave it."

We both laughed, and just like that, Tony and I were friends. Exactly as foretold.

We told dumb jokes. Laughed about the grudges we used to hold. Then Tony blurted out, "I love you." Which caught me off guard and brought tears to my eyes.

I was thankful. So thankful. Thankful to God that Tony got to hear me say, "I love you too."

Not long after, Tony couldn't work anymore. He and his brother were carpenters, but the treatment wore him down.

On more than one Sunday, I'd sneak out early, find Tony's car, and tuck a hundred-dollar bill into the steering wheel. Then I'd wait across the parking lot and watch him through my rear-view mirror as he discovered it.

He'd whip around, trying to catch whoever did it—but never saw me watching. That was the point. I wanted God to get the credit. But still... watching Tony bow his head in grateful silence? That was my blessing.

Six months later, almost to the day—Tony died.

I thanked God that he didn't let that man die while I had the hate in my heart.

I had come to realize—I just hadn't known the real Tony.

CHAPTER ELEVEN

BETTER DAYS COMING

After taking them through some of his most painful memories—especially the part about Vu no longer by his side—Nghia changed the subject.

One of the most frightening part, he recalled, was not just the American artillery but the sight of fellow PAVN soldiers dying on the Truong Son range.

"B-52s flying high overhead—no one heard them—suddenly soldiers vaporized before my eyes."

Entire regiments vanishing into clouds of dust—scenes that haunted him. Vu watched his eyes. Tears began forming, and before they dropped, she reached to wipe them from his face, hoping to erase some of his memories, but she knew from experience that might not be possible.

As much as Nghia wanted to forget, he brought home things that cut deep. Nguyen Van Ba, his younger brother and a favorite among his siblings, died in the fighting at Kontum. As far as Nghia knew, Ba's remains were never recovered. No proper burial, no ceremony, no posthumous medals. Just gone—melted into the jungle or turned to mist by massive bombs.

Honoring family tradition, Nghia lit several candles and stared at the flames until they disappeared. He told Vu he would not hold a grudge against those who took his brother's life. Vu understood that heartache. She'd known her own. Of eleven brothers and sisters, she was one of only two who survived starvation during the Japanese occupation in World War II—unfathomable even by Vietnamese standards.

Once the candles gave way to the night and the children were safely in bed, Nghia and Vu lay down, confident that the sun would rise on a new day.

At dawn, as light spilled through the banana trees, Nghia and Vu sipped tea when a man from the local People's Committee approached.

"Good morning, are you Nguyen Van Nghia?" he asked.

"I am," Nghia replied.

The man introduced himself as To Quang Hang, of the Tien Hai People's Committee. Nghia had a pending court date. The court was giving him an opportunity to secure identity papers and begin medical treatment and receive his pension.

Vu spoke up. "That's good news."

"What kind of evidence does the court need?" Nghia asked.

"Birth records, family documents, photos—anything that proves who you are."

Vu shook her head. "The typhoon last year flooded our home. We lost everything."

To Quang remained silent as he departed. He was just the messenger.

Not long after Nghia's return, in the dark of night, Vu had once roused him and the children after hearing the loudspeaker's warning that American bombers were enroute. They ran in pitch darkness as a bomber roared overhead.

"Those barbarians," Nghia muttered. "We are only a small country. Why must they bully us this way?"

Vu had no answer. "We must get to safety before they kill us all."

They reached the shelters—earthen bunkers built at the start of the war. Vu stood at the door, ushering the children inside before entering herself.

Nghia had been in bunkers before—back in Kontum with his men—but never like this. This time, he was a broken man. His wife and children huddled around him, trying to comfort him while the ground shook with bombs.

He asked, "Vu, how did you know to run?"

"The Russians," she said. "They have ships off the coast of Okinawa and Guam. Spotters in Thailand radio Hanoi when bombers take off. The loudspeakers warn us. We usually have enough time." She added that she and the children had run to this shelter many times—three times in one night, even.

This time, with his family at his side, the memories of bunkers on Cherry Hill came flooding back. Once again, Nghia turned to poetry. He whispered to Vu that he had written a poem about her flute during one of his darkest days in the South. Dirt fell from the walls around them as bombs shattered the earth nearby.

"I wrote it as a conversation between us," he said. Then he began:

THE FLUTE

Last night beside the fire, I stayed up all
night. I made this flute for you, my love.

Until we meet again, may you see my face
each time you play. Remember our promises
to remain forever faithful. I can see you
playing the flute constantly. Though far
apart, you will always be waiting for me.

My love, you joined the army to serve your
country. Troubled, I yet advised you to

> *defend your native land. We embrace, oh my dear. Never embrace another. Please always remember the flute you gave me. Remember our promises to remain forever faithful. Though far apart, I will always be waiting for you. I stand here in the rice fields at day's end; mist clouds the horizon.*
>
> *My little flute melody has been carried off by the wind. It is for the one I love miles and miles away. The rice shouts with glee in the fields. The blooming flowers renew my hope. I sew this shirt with my love to send to my faraway soldier. Though far apart, I will always be waiting for you. I am always with you.*

Vu clutched his hand. "We only know the bombs are falling. We don't know if we'll live to love again. But even now, they haven't shaken your memory of me."

The loudspeaker blared again—the bombers had left. It was safe.

At sunrise, they surveyed their home and found no damage. But just a few hundred meters away, a military installation lay in ruins—bomb craters, collapsed buildings. Somehow, the People's Committee building had survived.

As Nghia's court date approached, he and Vu focused on what they'd need to bring.

Then Vu had an idea. "Maybe your old unit can verify your identity."

Nghia hesitated. "The war's still going on. They're still fighting the Americans."

Still, the next morning, she helped him into a wagon full of rice stalks headed toward his old base. The building was there. The surroundings were familiar, but there were no soldiers. A man answered the door.

"I'm acting regimental Colonel Han," he said. "How can I help you?"

Vu explained their situation. "Nghia was wounded and without ID and needs proof to receive care."

Colonel Han narrowed his eyes. "Is that so?" He studied Nghia.

"Then tell me—how can he be here, alive, while the war continues? There are only three ways a soldier escapes fighting! He claims to have fought the Americans, where many of our countrymen became martyrs. And yet he stands here!"

Vu, realizing this was a mistake, ripped open her husband's shirt, revealing the wounds. "When he was wounded, they took him to an underground hospital. They didn't think he'd survive. These wounds are what he gave for his country. He cannot work. He cannot provide. Isn't that enough?"

She asked Nghia to remove his pants, revealing the wound to his leg—almost an amputation.

"Doctors thought he would die on the Truong Son range. I don't know how he made it back. But now he's here. And they won't treat him unless he has the papers he lost in Kontum," she said.

The colonel paused. "Let me check the unit roster."

He returned with news. "According to our records, Nguyen Van Nghia died in Kontum in 1968."

Vu nodded. "Yes. Military men came to my work and told me he was dead. I mourned him. But two years later, he showed up at our village."

Colonel Han studied the scar above Nghia's left eyebrow. It matched the record.

"Very well," he said. "I'll give you documentation for the court."

Nghia got his new identification papers. He began medical treatment and received his pension. During his first medical exam, doctors discovered vision loss—one eye nearly gone, the other not far behind.

The doctor lowered his gaze and said quietly, "We don't have the training or equipment to treat it."

Nghia nodded, as if he'd expected it. After everything, even the gift of seeing, the world again was slipping away—one eye at a time.

CHAPTER TWELVE

TRANSLATED

Homeless and penniless now, I didn't realize I was suffering from PTSD—post-traumatic stress disorder—an emotional condition first labeled by the Veterans' Administration (VA) as the Vietnam Syndrome. Before that, in the Civil War, it was called Soldier's Heart; in WWI, it was called Shell Shock; and in WWII and Korea, it was called Battle Fatigue—yet the symptoms were basically the same. However, during the latter part of the Vietnam War and afterward, the Vietnam Syndrome label was replaced with PTSD.

Whatever the label, its effects were disruptive. In high school, I took mechanical drafting and made straight A's. My instructor said I ought to be a graphics engineer or architect. My drawing ability was good. That had been before PTSD. But this was now. Sitting still was a requirement for draftsmen, engineers, or architects—and returning to the mindset of my high school days was no longer possible.

It was Independence Day, 1989, when I took a friend to the Cotton Bowl for the annual Fourth of July fireworks. We arrived early and saw a large display near the front gates—red Texas granite blocks stacked on a plywood platform. Hundreds, maybe thousands, of names were carved into the stone. It was the Texas Vietnam Veterans Memorial, soon to be officially dedicated on Veterans Day.

I didn't bother looking for names. I didn't care to. I didn't want to. Let the others search for their ghosts—I had enough ghosts of my own. I just stood there, empty, hollow, trying to stay numb.

But then it came, sudden and merciless, slamming into me like a steel beam to the skull. My chest buckled, my gut twisted, and everything I thought was buried came roaring back. Rage, grief, shame, guilt—layer after layer of it—swarming me, choking me, clawing on me from the inside out. I couldn't stop it. Couldn't hold it down. It tore through me, left me bleeding in ways no one could see, raw and filthy, as if the war itself had followed me to the fairground and would never let me go.

My chest constricted as if an elephant were sitting on it. I gasped for air as tears streamed uncontrollably down my face. I turned and ran—no idea where I was going or what I was doing. Vietnam came flooding back. Standing at the wall shattered what little was left of my mental stability.

When my friend caught up, I couldn't even explain what was happening. It was like reliving the war all over again, like a videotape playing the worst scenes of my life. Not just images or sound—but everything.

I remembered the nightly television coverage. The protests. The politicians talking about the "domino effect." I remembered the dying—casualties reported on the evening news, discussed like sports scores.

After that, the war consumed me. The counselors at the vet center said the more I talked about it, the less it would control me. I even started speaking at high schools and universities whose textbooks barely mentioned the war. But no matter how much I talked, Vietnam stayed with me.

I learned PTSD didn't just come from war. Trauma came in many forms. But the one common thread—whatever caused it—was memory. Memory that wouldn't let go.

One night, over dinner, I told a story from the war. My mom got a strange look on her face and left the table. She returned with the C-ration box I'd sent home nearly twenty years earlier.

"Here's something you sent us. Do you remember it?" she asked.

I stared at the box for a long time. "Where's it been all these years?"

"In the attic," she called from the kitchen. "Under a bunch of old luggage."

Dad chimed in, "I had seen it too, but assumed it was trash."

"That's not what it is," Mom said, pointing to the return address.

I took a breath and lifted the lid. The stench hit me like a wave—jungle rot, sweat ground into fabric, the sweet-sick reek of charred flesh, the crawling stench of maggots, death itself. War smells. They rushed at me, dragging memories up too fast, too many, all at once. My stomach heaved, my hands shook, and I slammed the lid shut before it swallowed me whole.

Afraid to sleep, I kept the lights on. Finally, exhaustion overtook me.

Days later, I sat alone in the dark, staring at the box. I wanted to open it again. But I didn't. Leaving it shut meant avoiding what was inside.

Later, I spotted the box on my desk again. With more courage this time, I opened the top flaps. The same rush of memories hit me like shrapnel. I closed it again.

That night, I lay in bed, staring at the ceiling. Then I got up and opened the box for real. Everything was still there. Photos. Stamps. Money. And the small, fake alligator skin-covered book, still speckled with dried dirt.

Not ammo. Not maps. Not coordinates. These were human things—kept close for reasons no war could explain. I took the book out and placed it on the nightstand, waiting to see if it would trigger anything. It didn't, so I opened it. I saw nothing but beautiful Vietnamese handwriting. Words I couldn't read.

Later, my mom peeked in and saw me thumbing through it.

"Do you know what it says?" she asked.

I snapped, "It's in Vietnamese, Mom."

She didn't take it personally. She knew I was struggling. No job, no car, no house—a feeling like I was at the bottom of the ocean under whale defecation. But she still believed something better was coming.

She offered an idea. "If it were me, I'd get it translated. There might be something in there that could help you. Maybe you could write a book."

I told her I was a truck driver, not a writer. And nothing any enemy soldier wrote could help me.

Still, I started asking questions. "What's his name? Where's he from?"

Mom found what looked like a name, "Nguyen Van Nghia," she spelled out slowly.

We both butchered the pronunciation with our Texas drawl.

There were photos, one of a boy on his mother's lap and another of a girl, maybe his sister. And a woman, probably his wife. Suddenly, I realized I was holding the entire life story of an enemy soldier. Previously, I thought I was holding the scraps of a nameless foot soldier.

But mixed in with the photos and poems were other pages—official ones. Typed. Stamped. Signed. They did not speak in the language of love. They spoke in the language of a state at war.

One bore a round seal in red ink. Another carried a formal signature line. I didn't know it then, but those markings placed Nguyen Van Nghia inside the machinery of North Vietnam's army—not at the margins, but at its center.

Years later, I would learn what those pages meant. They were promotion orders issued by the Ministry of National Defense of the Democratic Republic of Vietnam. Centrally authorized. Not a field scribble. Not a local favor. The kind of document reserved for men being entrusted with command. Nguyen Van Nghia had been commissioned as an officer.

The stamp belonged to the 24th Regiment of the 304th Division—one of the North Vietnamese Army's most storied formations. An elite unit. A front-line regiment sent into the hardest corridors of the war—Route 9, Khe Sanh, Quảng Trị. Places where men disappeared by the hundreds. Places they built to grind boys into ghosts.

The same hand that wrote "Love bears no grudge" had been trained to lead men through those killing grounds.

That knowledge didn't soften the poems. It made them heavier. They meant this man had stood inside the war's engine and still written about tenderness. That he had carried authority, duty, and blood—and still left room in his soul for love.

Of course, I didn't know that at the time. All I knew—the enemy was beginning to look dangerously human.

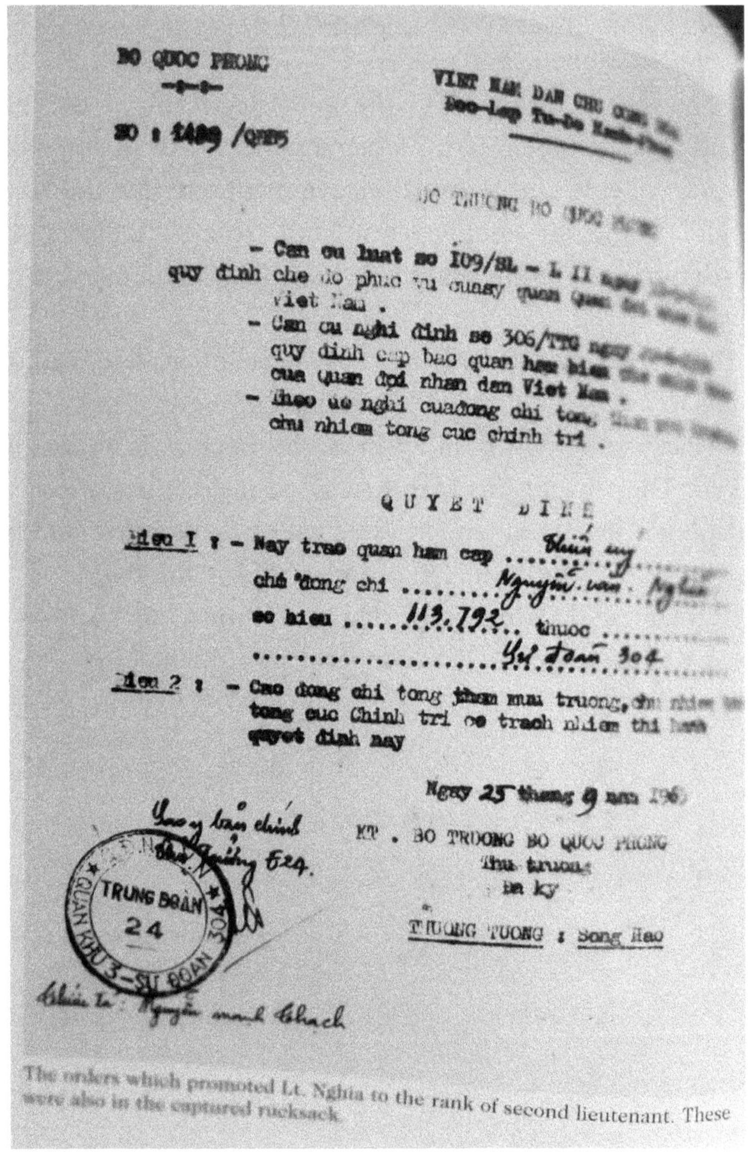

BO QUOC PHONG
-*-*-
SO : [illegible] /QĐ65

VIET NAM DAN CHU CONG HOA
Doc-Lap Tu-Do Hanh-Phuc

BO TRUONG BO QUOC PHONG

- Can cu luat so 109/SL - L 11 ngay [illegible] quy dinh che do phuc vu cua sy quan quan doi nhan dan Viet Nam.
- Can cu nghi dinh so 306/TTG ngay [illegible] quy dinh cap bac quan ham [illegible] cua quan doi nhan dan Viet Nam.
- Theo de nghi cua dong chi tong [illegible] chu nhiem tong cuc chinh tri.

QUYET DINH

Dieu I : - Nay trao quan ham cap .... Thiếu úy ....
cho dong chi .... Nguyễn văn Nghĩa ....
so hieu .... 113.792 .... thuoc ....
.... Sư đoàn 304 ....

Dieu 2 : - Cac dong chi tong tham muu truong, chu nhiem tong cuc Chinh tri co trach nhiem thi hanh quyet dinh nay

Ngay 25 thang 9 nam 196[illegible]

KT. BO TRUONG BO QUOC PHONG
Thu truong
Da ky
THUONG TUONG : Song Hao

Sao y bản chính
Chỉ huy Trưởng E24.

TRUNG ĐOÀN 24
QUÂN KHU 3 - SƯ ĐOÀN 304

[illegible]: Nguyễn mạnh Thạch

The orders which promoted Lt. Nghia to the rank of second lieutenant. These were also in the captured rucksack.

Nghia's promotion order. Official promotion order issued by the Ministry of National Defense of the Democratic Republic of Vietnam, dated September 25, 1965, commissioning Nguyễn Văn Nghĩa as a Second Lieutenant in the People's Army of Vietnam.

Round red seal. Regimental seal of the 24th Regiment, 304th Division—one of the PAVN's most storied front-line units.

I became obsessed with the book. Holding the book, I remembered my hatred, rage, my isolation, and depression. My road rage in Wyoming—the shotgun. The sense that no one could ever understand. But as I read more about trauma—rape victims, survivors of abuse—I saw something shared. Different circumstances. Same soul damage.

For the first time since coming home, I began asking myself hard questions.

Why did I go to war? Was he really my enemy? Was the anger necessary? How did I have so much hatred toward a soldier, whom I'd never met, and who had never once done anything to me, except be born under a different flag, with orders of his own, in a war neither of us started?

Too many questions.

Like my mother once said, anger helped me survive in Vietnam. It kept me alive. It was part of the training. And I accepted that. But maybe she was right to wonder whether she'd lost her son the day I lost that innocence.

Her idea of translating the small book started to make sense. I bought a Vietnamese-English dictionary and tried my hand at decoding it. I even went to a Vietnamese restaurant and asked the owner for help. He read a little, but clearly didn't want to get involved, especially when they found out the author of the little book was from the north.

I placed an ad for a translator. Four responded. One didn't start. Another didn't finish. The rest fizzled out.

Then I heard about Vinh. He was Vietnamese. Former ARVN. A refugee, like so many others. I thought maybe he could help. At first, he resisted. "This man—he enemy. Hard to read what he writes. I hate him."

Weeks passed, but I kept pushing. I was desperate. I needed to know—was this man a monster? Or something else?

Eventually, Vinh agreed—on one condition. If his name was left out of the Vietnamese community, he would do the translation. When we met again, he was sweating bullets. Finally, he spoke.

"The man who write this is... good man."

I exploded. "You call him a good man?"

"Yes," Vinh said, "I don't like it either. But I must tell true. He even... family man. He is well respected in his village. They even call him Uncle he is so well revered. "

My blood pressure skyrocketed. Vinh had to be wrong. Either he misread it, or he was lying. He was from the same country. Maybe that made him the enemy, too.

Vinh offered the translation, but I jerked away. Then I took it and stormed off.

After I wadded up and wrinkled what Vinh wrote, I tossed it under books, tapes, and junk mail on my desk.

Forgotten.

Later, I sat outside under the old tree I used to climb as a boy. I spent hours wondering how I lost my family, house, job, and all I'd worked so hard for.

I remembered my dad saying I'd have to earn my way through life, and that's the way I was, an achiever. And still, I was back here, under the tree.

I believed in God, but I was angry about losing everything my hard work had produced, and that had been so hard to achieve.

A friend once told me that people blame God when they don't want to take responsibility for how they ended up. It hit me hard. But I still blamed Him.

One afternoon, I snapped. Not at anyone, not even myself. Just rage. I raised my fist to heaven and screamed, "Why? Why have you done this to me?"

Before I could breathe, I heard an answer.

"I was exactly where I was supposed to be."

Hard as that was to believe, the message calmed me. Hearing from God that quickly was something I'd never experienced before.

Someone once said everything happens by design. I didn't know what that meant—but if it applied to me, I'd take it. I realized I was in a new place—one I'd never been before. Not physically, but spiritually.

On my desk sat junk mail, cassette tapes, and paperbacks I hadn't touched in months. At the bottom of the pile—Vinh's translation.

Sometimes, God has to turn your eyes away from what's right in front of you—so you'll finally look up. To receive something new, you've got to let go of what you already have. Even if it means losing everything? "Yes," the voice said, "It will be worth it."

Even with that comfort, I still had questions. Where do I go now? What can I possibly do, broken like this?

Then the desk called out—not with sound, but with weight. I stepped closer, not knowing what—if anything—was about to happen. But down deep inside, intuitively, I knew something was changing.

The translation was crude, like Vinh explained. Not so much a surprise, but while smoothing out the wrinkles, I became intrigued—the writing looked like poetry. After counting the pages and finding a total of twenty-six, I went back for a closer look.

What I saw earlier left me hoping I was in the midst of a very bad dream and that everything happening was only make-believe, and that I'd wake up soon.

Either Vinh's translation was one big fat lie—or a huge mistake. I didn't know which. Yet, as I flipped the pages one by one, I'd find out soon enough what Vinh had done.

In several places, I spotted familiar words like civilian, enemy, country, wife, brother—even uncle. A little further in, I read words like home, mother, dad, and even soldier.

That was impossible, enemy soldiers did not—could not—even use such words, let alone know their meaning. Besides, those were human words, and only humans knew and understood them.

By now, I was certain I was being scammed—tricked into believing something good about the enemy. The translator was trying to make Vietnamese people look good with poetry. "That had to be it," I told myself—a test to see if I'd fall for the lie that enemies were human.

Even as I encountered such questions, I continued thumbing through the pages until I landed on the last page. At the top of the page, one word—the title of a poem. One word shouldn't cause anyone to blow his top, but this one did.

Anger deep inside, boiling over like molten lava, ready to blow, sent me into a frenzy. I bounced from wall to wall and off the ceiling, screaming, "No! No! No! This can't be true!"

Polly heard it and came running. "What's wrong?" What's wrong?" she pleaded frantically, tapping on my door. Hearing her rat-tat-tat-rat-tat-tat on the door sounded too familiar—like a machine gun in the jungle—so I wasn't about to answer.

I didn't predict that kind of response, but stored inside me and encased in an almost impenetrable barrier, was a difficult disease—hatred.

When I finally opened up, I was in a tangled web, engulfed by memories of war and surrounded by a dark aura. I said nothing. Polly noticed that I was holding the wrinkled translation.

"Is that what the man wrote?" she asked, pointing to my hand.

"Yeah, but I haven't finished reading. It's just too much to stomach," I told her.

She was surprised to hear me say that, since I'd gone to so much trouble getting the small book, the little volume that seemed to travel with me not just in my pocket but through my life, translated. "It's just a lot of lies, Mom. The translator's got down here things that are impossible." Thinking she'd be offended like me, I said, "Looks like he wrote poetry, Mom."

She wanted to know what was so offensive. Soldiers on the battlefield were always lonely, writing stuff like that. She'd seen it in war movies.

I gazed at her with a look of vengeance. Didn't she know the enemy was nothing more than a killer? Something subhuman? I felt as though she was siding with the enemy instead of me.

"Mom, look," I said, tossing the translation to the floor, "I'm not gonna read it. You should understand," raising my voice almost high enough for the neighbors to hear, "We were enemies.

We fought in the stinking jungle. He'd kill me just as easily as I'd kill him. They weren't even people. Just rats—little animals crawling in holes and trees. They'd pop up out of a hole, shoot one of us, then dive underground and out of sight. We hated that. We hated them."

"Besides," I went on, referring to one of the poems that angered me most—and again thinking she'd be just as revolted as I was, "There's one in there titled 'Love.' Love ain't for enemy guys," I shouted. "It's for us, humans."

Polly was a loving person. She'd always tried to teach her son to be loving, too, and she loved me. But she'd never seen this dark side. My angry war side. She had never gone through training. She'd never been in a war, never seen death. She didn't understand. She didn't have to. She understood things about life, love, and family—and she was quick-witted enough to know how to respond to her angry son.

Polly snatched the translation from the floor and, before sitting down, asked me to make coffee. By the time I got back, she had read every poem—and loved them.

Long ago, intuition had guided her during dinner the night she suggested I have the little book translated, its presence steady, as though it waited to be opened when the time was right. Her perception had told her that something in the little book was meant for me.

After reading it for herself, her perceptions were verified. She'd been right all along. Inside, she didn't find a subhuman creature or little animal, but a man with an acute awareness of life, family, duty, and country. His writing was profound.

She understood the power behind the writing—the power of love. Now, if only she could become an instrument in God's hands. She believed those tiny pages held enough power to help her son conquer a hatred beyond anything measurable. She'd always believed the little journal was heaven-sent. Now, her desire was to help the love she read on paper transfer into my heart and move me from darkness to light. From hate to love.

She heard me coming down the hall, but before I came in, she said a quick prayer.

"Seems he had," she said, speaking of the former enemy, "written this in the face of death. It's poetry about his loneliness, fear, anger, duty, hope, and love for his country. It appears he had a lot of love for friends and love for his family."

Staring me in the eye, she asked, "Isn't that what you had—for us, your family, your country, your friends—love?"

I stood in silence, trying to think of an answer, but before I could say anything, she began reading aloud the one poem that had angered me most, starting with the title.

LOVE

Love bears no grudge.
It is not a butterfly and flower.
Love endures until old age.
Do not trifle with love, or there will be sorrow.
Do not rush love in order to enjoy it.
Handle love with care;
Be compromising.
Close your eyes, forget about everything.
Calm yourself, listen to the world speak.
Love bears no grudge.

She paused for a moment... and in that pause, something shifted. I'd never viewed my mother as a trigger before—but that's exactly what she had become. And she triggered me as nothing had before.

She continued. Her voice sounded sweet—a pleasurable sound, resonating like an angel whispering in my ear. She spoke

Nghia's words, but at that moment, it wasn't his voice I heard. It was God's.

For a long time, I carried the war inside me. Not just the memories… but the image of the enemy. It had been burned into me—trained into me—reinforced in the heat of battle. The enemy was not a man. Not someone with a family. Not someone who loved. Just the enemy. And I held onto that. Tight. Because letting it go felt like betrayal. Betrayal of the men we lost. Betrayal of what we had endured.

There were moments—quiet ones—when something in me would begin to question it. A crack. Just a small one. And every time… I pushed it back down. I wasn't ready. Didn't want to be. But the diary wouldn't leave me alone. Those words… that poem… they kept coming back. Not loud. Not demanding. Just there. Waiting.

There came a moment—I remember it clearly—when I felt it again. That pressure. That question rising up from somewhere deep inside me. I could feel the old anger tightening. Holding. Resisting. And then… something shifted. Not outside of me. Inside. It wasn't a voice I could explain. Not something I could point to. But it was real. And it stopped me. Right there… in the middle of it.

I stood there, caught between what I had always believed… and what I was beginning to see. That maybe… the line I had drawn between us…wasn't as real as I thought. That beneath the uniforms… the training… the war… we were not as different as I had been taught to believe. That somehow—across all of it—there was a kind of oneness… not in what we had done… but in who we were. Men.

Human beings trying to survive something neither of us had created. And for the first time… I didn't push it away. I let it stay. And in that moment—without fully understanding how or why—I took the first step toward forgiveness.

Not just for him. For me. Forgiving him was like being handed the keys to the jailhouse door I didn't even realize I'd been locked behind. And when I finally opened it, it felt like the weight of the whole world came off my shoulders. I could finally breathe again.

I felt that I was coming home at last—home not of the earth, but of peace. The home I ached for, the one I thought I'd never have or know. Heaven was real, and for the first time in my life, I was standing right on its threshold.

And there was my son, Silas—waiting—watching—smiling, ready to know the man his dad could finally be. Ever since that revelation hit me, we've had a life together. One I never thought I'd get to live. Not just morose days, not just survival, but joy, laughter, adventures, and most of all LOVE.

Because, for the first time since I returned from Vietnam... he has the dad he always wanted, and I get to be that dad.

The man I needed to be... before the war took him from me.

Later, when my mother and father talked about what had happened—about the diary, about the change in me—my father said something I've never forgotten, "There's a time to kill… and a time to heal. A time for war, and a time for peace."

I knew where he had taken it from, Ecclesiastes in the bible. Ancient words that had outlived empires and wars long before ours.

For years, my life had been trapped in one season—the season of killing and surviving. But somewhere between a mother's obedience to a whisper… and a poem written in a jungle by a man I once called enemy… the season shifted.

Not by accident. Not by coincidence. By design.

The same God who allows a time for war also appoints a time for healing. And when that time comes, no man can hold it back.

The diary did not find me late. It found me right on time. And I finally stepped into the season that had been waiting for me all along.

CHAPTER THIRTEEN

OFF TO THE COUNSELOR

Somewhere before the end of the poem, my mom experienced a flashback of her own regarding the day the C-ration box arrived. Why did it come? She didn't know. What was it there for? She hadn't a clue. But before she'd finished reading the poem titled "Love," she had her answer.

She'd been chosen—perhaps for one of the most difficult tasks of her life. She was to shine a light on her son's disease—hatred. It was her calling, carried out with help from what came to her doorstep years earlier in a box. And then, right before her eyes, the transformation appeared—inevitable, undeniable, as though fate itself had chosen the moment.

There was no mistaking it—the little book had remained hidden in the box, patient, as though it knew only to emerge at the perfect moment, when her son needed it most. Polly got the reassurance she'd been looking for—all things happen according to God's perfect timing.

My mother believed love was the one and only thing the Creator of our world and the universe actually ever created—and it was like glue holding everything together. Without love, everything simply falls apart.

"There's nothing above the level of love. It is the highest power or energy in the universe, and there was nothing it could not overcome," she said.

Suddenly, the meaning of the poem titled "Love" came into full view. Nghia's words broke hatred's stronghold over me. His words opened something I didn't know was closed. Listening to my mom eased me, but I still couldn't stop reminiscing about the past. I tried to think back to when the so-called truth I adhered to for decades turned out to be nothing more than a lie, but nothing came close.

The hardest truth was this—the enemy I saw back then as only a target—something inhuman—had been human all along. Facing that truth was both bitter and sweet.

And maybe that truth isn't only about war. Maybe it speaks to us here and now, in the ordinary battles of daily life, divorces, harsh bosses, broken friendships, or neighbors we can't forgive. How often do we, without even noticing, strip away another's humanity because they look different, believe differently, or come from the "other side"?

It's easier to see them as enemies than to see them as real people, humans. But the truth is unshakable—they love, they suffer, they hope, they fear, and they put on their clothes—just as we do. Isn't that what Scripture keeps reminding us? *That we are one body, though many parts.* That the dividing walls of hostility have been broken down, we all bleed red. We finally see the image of God in another—even in someone we once called an enemy—we begin to glimpse the oneness God intended from the beginning.

I was forced to admit that Vinh had told the truth, but now I suffered a pain of a different nature. With the realization that enemies were as human as I and we were more alike than not, new and more complex issues grieved me.

It was one thing to kill something seen as a subhuman—perhaps a by-peddler, or any of the names commonly used to de-humanize enemies—but it's an entirely different thing to kill a human. The truth was bitter—I'd swallowed a lie as if it were truth. But it was sweet too—because in the end, it meant I hadn't killed another human being.

The war had taken a great deal from me—friends, years, innocence, sleep. It had rearranged my mind and hollowed places in my chest I didn't know how to reach. But sitting there, listening to my mother, something else became clear. That war hadn't taken everything. There were things it could not destroy.

By now, my head was spinning. The first thing I did the next morning, after all the revelations, was reach for Vinh's translation—as if holding it might steady me, might make sense of everything that had just been revealed.

I held it close all the way to the Veterans Center, where vets could go to talk about what was on their minds. Upon my arrival, a counselor invited me into his office. I told him the story—how I packed a little chronicle or memoir book away in a C-ration box and sent it to my folks.

The counselor told me it was the first time he'd ever heard a story like mine. Still, he welcomed it, glad I was finally opening up, and he listened with full attention, every word from beginning to end.

"You mean this box?" He pointed to the photo, "This is the same box your mom kept in a dark attic for nearly twenty years? Then, when you moved in with your parents, she retrieved it from the attic and gave it to you a couple of decades later. Is that what you are saying?"

"That's exactly what I'm saying."

Then, opening up as I'd never done with anyone before, I told him about the experience that I had intended to keep to myself.

I said, *"Look... when my mom read me a poem from the enemy's writings... I don't even know how to put this into words. Her voice...it wasn't just hers anymore. It hit me hard, like something pure cutting straight through to my soul. Honestly, it sounded like an angel speaking to me. And I didn't know what to do with that."*

"I'm curious," the man asked. "Which one of the enemy poems did your mom read out loud?"

"The one titled, "Love."

Hearing that struck a chord with the man. After pausing quietly for a second, he spoke up, "Actually, I've heard most of my adult life that God is love."

A reverent man and Vietnam veteran himself, he knew enough about the man sitting in his office to acknowledge something of great consequence had happened inside him—but he didn't really know what.

"There's got to be an explanation," the man said after hearing all the details of the story. "I think it goes like this, scratching his head, there's some kind of connection between the enemy guy's poem called "Love" and God, since God is love. Maybe that is the reason why your mom's voice sounded angelic."

My mind was going haywire, latching onto every word the counselor said. "Go on," I said.

"Most people make God too small—like He only fits inside a box. But here's how I see it. He was in the poem. He was in the box. He was in the attic, waiting. Waiting for the day you'd step into your parents' house, so He could meet you there.

"Let me walk it through, step by step," he said gently.

"First, the box. Well, let me back up a little, going a little deeper. First, there was the enemy. What or who was inside him, getting him to compose that poem? Then, you captured his little book, er, ah, his journal, or whatever you want to call it—you then put it inside the box." After a pause, he continued, "Second—you put that box on a chopper bound for home. Third—it ended up in your mother's attic, sealed away, waiting in the dark. Fourth—years went by, life came apart, PTSD dogged your every step, and you found yourself back under your parents' roof. Fifth—your mom pulled out that little book and read a poem aloud. Sixth—

those words broke through like clean air after smoke, and her voice came across as if an angel were speaking.

"That's a chain of events, man.. Enemy. Battle. Book. Box. Attic. Timing. Voice. Each link holds. So, I don't think this is small or random. I think God was present in every step—breathing words into the enemy soldier's hand, guarding the enemy ledger in the dark, and choosing the hour it would open for you.

"And that's why it landed so hard. Probably why you lost all your earthly possessions and became homeless. Not because you were losing it, but because you were being found. Seen. Met right when and where you needed the revelation most. And as if that wasn't enough, He kept you alive all these years to discover all this."

With a look of amazement, I said, "I don't completely understand your thinking, or how you came to all those conclusions, but speaking in those terms, it sounds like you are correct."

The counselor continued, "They—they being most people—speaking of God—keep Him confined and enclosed until they need Him. That's when they let Him out of the boxes they have kept him in. But get this—they don't let him out until they need him, or because of some trouble they've gotten themselves into, and they don't know how to get out. The rest of the time, they keep him locked away in some dark, dusty ole attic.

"Did ya get that, Reed? In your case, you had Him in a box—and He waited for nearly two decades for you to realize your need. Then suddenly, when you opened the box, He ambushed you. He got out and all over you.

"Hey, you got ambushed when you least expected it."

Still trying to piece it all together, I liked how the counselor put it in terms I could understand. "Ambushed, huh?" I agreed because that was how it all appeared.

The man continued, "God is like that. He is so big He will let people put him in a box just to surprise them once they discover they need Him.

"Now here's something that I'll bet you hadn't thought about, and when you get hold of this, it will totally blow your mind. You didn't really know what you were doing that day in Kontum when you went through the backpack of an enemy soldier—and stuffed all his things in a C-ration box. It sounded as though those things were just something to send home—maybe proof you'd been there, as you had no idea what he was really carrying.

"But God knew. He knew from the moment you flipped through that tiny book that you'd be sending it home in a box—and that buried inside was a poem named "Love," a poem that one day would become your key to healing.

"Looking back, you believed it wasn't random. It wasn't luck. It was something holy. God had known all along what you would need—long before the war broke you, long before you even knew you needed healing. God had planted it there, inside that box, waiting for the moment when your heart would be ready to see the enemy as a fellow human being. And not just that—but as a mirror.

"This is perhaps larger than life—you had to be stripped of all your earthly possessions so He could get your attention—because you were too busy to even slow down. Otherwise, you probably would not have moved in with your parents as a homeless man—and probably would not have been given the C-ration box that had waited for you in their attic nearly two decades—and possibly denying you the powerful lessons you are learning.

"You need to be thankful you became homeless in the first place, man. One poem, simply titled "Love," struck like shrapnel to your soul. It wasn't filled with hate or propaganda. It was about a woman. Tender. Personal. Vulnerable. The enemy, it turned out, had a heart. Had a wife. Had poetry.

"That's when your heart broke wide open. Some might call it a coincidence. God called it grace, wrapped in a C-ration box." Having finished his expose, he sat back seemingly amazed at his own words.

I said, "A good friend of mine, Mr. Dale Doucet from Louisiana, suggested I should search out and find his wife and give her the little book. Do you really believe God knew all that stuff in advance and let the little book stay in a box in a dark attic for two decades just to help me—and possibly others?"

The counselor responded in a way that gave me a lot of hope.

"Why, heck yeah, I do. I'm going to guarantee you this one thing," the counselor said. "God is bigger than any ole box. A lot bigger. Why do you think your mom told you to get that small book translated? It's because she knew.

"Think back to when you were in the jungle searching those backpacks. Did you have any idea that your hatred for the enemy would be reversed by a few words of love written in a tiny journal?"

I didn't want to admit hating that badly, but the counselor was right as rain. I hated the enemy and carried that hatred for decades, letting it fester inside me. I even hated non-enemies of Vietnamese descent who had fought on the same side as the Americans.

Then the counselor said, "Once God got out of the box, He did a number on your heart. He used something as simple as words written in a foreign language to transform you into someone who will never hate again. If that is not a huge God, I don't know what is.

"Besides everything we've spoken of here today, getting rid of hate is a good thing. Hate is an emotional problem, but it has a way of leaking over into our physical bodies and can cause all kinds of sicknesses.

"I bet you didn't know that, did ya? I'm glad for you, man. Hey, let me run something past you, okay? You don't have to do it, but it's something for you to think about. I'm not saying you have to do this, but earlier, you mentioned that a man named Doucet suggested you take the book to your former enemy's wife. What do you think about his suggestion?"

I interrupted, "Yes, Doucet understood the significance of Vietnamese tradition. He told me, 'That book's full of poems about her. If she's alive, she needs to have it. Families over there don't move around as they do here. You could find her. The war's over. You could go.' At first, the idea of returning to Vietnam turned my stomach. But he definitely planted a seed."

I didn't know at the time if a trip would come together, or if I could even find her. But I knew one thing beyond doubt—everything I'd taken from his pack, his photos, flags, and the little book etched in that beautiful handwriting—belonged with her, not me.

Months later, Steve Smith, a documentary filmmaker from Seattle, caught wind of my desire to return the captured enemy's personal things, including his thoughts in a little book, to the wife of the soldier I may have killed in Kontum.

Smith drafted a one-page summary describing his plan to escort and film a veteran, Mr. Paul Reed, returning captured war items to the wife of a deceased PAVN officer. He sent it to the Ministry of Foreign Affairs (MOFA) in Hanoi. A young officer named Luong Thanh Nghi read it and pushed it to his superiors, hoping to get it approved. Diplomatic relations between the U.S. and Vietnam hadn't yet resumed, so permission to film inside the country was no small task.

But the Ministry found the project meaningful and quickly gave it the green light. Immediately, Steve sent copies of Nguyen Van Nghia's ID card, his promotion orders to lieutenant, and other documents—including enlarged photocopies of his complete, handwritten journal—that had been taken from his backpack in Kontum.

MOFA started searching for the family.

Smith got a call, "We've located the family."

He flew to Vietnam and, upon his return, called to update me.

"They found the family of Lieutenant Nguyen Van Nghia."

I paused. "Did they say anything about him? Is he—?"

"No mention," Smith said. "In Vietnam, when they say 'family,' it usually means brothers, sisters, children, uncles, aunts."

Then he dropped the bomb.

We were in Dallas, taping a final interview the day before the American Veterans Day. The camera was rolling. I was speaking calmly—just going through the motions, same old memories, well-worn lines when he said, "There's no easy way to tell you this... so I'll just say it. Nguyen Van Nghia is alive. And he wants to meet you."

Alive! I didn't speak. I didn't move. I just sat there, trying to breathe through it. It was as if the floor beneath me had tilted—gently at first, then all at once—and the weight I'd been carrying for twenty-five years shifted and landed somewhere I didn't know existed.

He was alive, which meant I hadn't killed him.

And that one thought hit harder than any shell I'd ever heard crack. I kept my face still, kept my posture steady. Smith said nothing more. The camera kept running. But inside—inside me there was something else entirely.

I realized in that moment, I'd spent a quarter century making peace with what I believed happened in that battle with Nghia's unit, and convinced myself that the man, whose backpack I'd taken containing all his personal items, had died. And that—I might've been the one who killed him.

Somehow, I was able to live with that because it was war. Because he was the enemy. Because he wasn't human. That's what we were taught. What we needed to believe. He wasn't someone's husband. He wasn't someone's father. He wasn't a poet. He wasn't real.

Until now. Now he was flesh and blood. Now he had a voice. A name and a will to meet me. With that single truth, everything rewrote itself. The guilt I'd buried deep—too deep to touch—rose up like smoke from a fire I thought I'd put out long ago. And with it came something I never expected. Relief! Unbearable, unspeakable relief.

Because I hadn't taken his life. He hadn't been erased from this world by my hand.

He was alive! And with that came a permission I didn't know I needed—to feel the full weight of what might have been—and to thank God it hadn't been so.

I swallowed hard. My hands rested quietly in my lap. My voice never cracked. But something deep inside me shifted. Like tectonic plates giving way after years of pressure.

And for the first time, I knew the enemy whose blood was not shed by my hand was the same enemy who had restored peace to my soul.

Always, my love, I miss your rosy cheeks.
Your boat has docked inside me forever.
Do you remember the quiet evenings—
The sunset on the water,
The wind tossing your hair?

The breaking waves laugh in time.
Perhaps the water can measure time.
Please keep track of our memories.

We said goodbye. Now we are apart.
The boat has taken my girl home.
That evening, my heart writhed in pain.

I love. I suffer.
Her boat still parts the evening waters.
Darling, forget me not.
Be happy during your spring years.

Be sad no longer,
Lest my heart irreparably break.
Always remember our promises—
To be faithful, and forever in love.

Our love is truly wondrous.
Our hair will turn gray together.
You smile. Your lips blossom
With hope for tomorrow.

Today, on the border, I take in the horizon,
Believing tomorrow will come.

—A poem by Lt. Nguyen Van Nghia

CHAPTER FOURTEEN

THE JOURNEY HOME

Twenty-five years after the Battle of Cherry Hill, in Tay Giang Village, Tien Hai District, early one morning, a young man approached a house believed to be the residence of former PAVN soldier Nguyen Van Nghia.

He was looking for a man who had fought in the American War.

"Ah, hello. Is this the residence of Nguyen Van Nghia?" the man asked. "Yes. Are you looking for me?"

"Yes. Please allow me to introduce myself. I'm Luong Thanh Nghi, an officer with the Ministry of Foreign Affairs in Hanoi."

"Oh, really? Your first name's close to mine," the man said. "Nghi instead of Nghia."

They chuckled. Then Nguyen Van Nghia understood the reason for the visit. "All right," he said. "I'll help you any way I can."

As the officer removed official-looking papers from his satchel, he said, "I'd like to ask you a few questions. Sir—I mean Mr. Nguyen—this document seems to be yours."

He held out photocopies of an identification card. "See? It lists your name, birth date, and place of birth."

"Yes, yes, I can see that," Mr. Nguyen replied, "but what do you need to know?"

"Well," Nghi said, "I'm trying to locate this man, but I need to be sure I've found the right person. Is this your identification card, sir?"

Although already suspicious, it wasn't his; Mr. Nguyen asked for a closer look. "It's my name, all right," he said, causing Nghi to perk up, "But the birth date isn't mine."

"This is not you?" Nghi asked, disappointed, wondering how he could have come to the wrong house.

"No, it's not me, sir." As Mr. Nguyen handed the paper back, he remarked that the man on the identification card had a scar on his forehead—just above his left eyebrow.

"Do you see a scar on my forehead, sir?"

Nghi glanced. There was no scar, even though the card said there should be. That meant only one thing—the young officer had the wrong Nguyen Van Nghia. Discouraged, Nghi pondered the thought for a moment, already dreading the long trip back to Hanoi.

Then, the man—who he'd hoped was the right one—asked, "Where did the identification papers come from?"

Nghi replied, "They belonged to a soldier who'd lost them during the American War."

Nguyen paused, then remembered, "There is another man, not far from here, who has the same name. In fact, I've heard the man fought in the south—on a battlefield in Kontum. But that was twenty-five years ago."

Nghi said, "Please, please, can you direct me to this man? Do you know where he lives?"

"I'm not positive," he replied, "But I heard he lives in another district of Tay Giang, near the main part of the village."

After asking a few locals—women pushing bicycles full of produce to market—Nghi learned the address of a wife, some children, and another man named Nguyen Van Nghia.

This was a critical moment for Nghi. If he didn't hurry, he'd be getting home after midnight, and he was a newlywed with a baby on the way. But he'd been given strict orders—don't return to the office until you find this Nguyen Van Nghia. Promotions at the ministry depended on it.

Before Nghi realized he'd gone to the wrong house, his emotions had already swung from excitement to disappointment. But now, with a solid lead, he was energized again, and it showed.

As he approached the house he'd been searching for all along, he noticed it had only one room. Fairly modern by Vietnamese standards, it had a small garden off to one side. It was midday. The sun was high, and the heat was thick. Most villagers were out in the rice fields—but here was a man, home. A man was working in the garden. He moved slowly, struggling a bit as he picked fruit. When he noticed Nghi watching, he stopped what he was doing and came over to greet the visitor, as was Vietnamese custom.

The Foreign Affairs officer asked his name. This time, Nghi waited for the answer before reaching into his satchel. The way Mr. Nguyen pronounced his full name matched the "uncle figure" Nghi had read about and imagined the night before.

"Very well, sir. This copy of an identification card bears your name. I previously located another man nearby with the same name—but it wasn't his birth date." Nghia let him know he was partially blind, so verifying the birth date in the small print wouldn't be easy, but he said he'd try.

"Do the best you can, sir... please tell me if this is your birth date."

He lifted the paper to his one good eye, not fully aware that his shaking hands would make reading almost impossible. The birth date was his, but Nghia couldn't speak.

"What's wrong?" Nghi asked. "Is this your identification card?"

But Nghia couldn't answer. Not in a way that would have given him credibility. He started to wobble like he'd had too much to drink. When he looked ready to fall, Nghi reached out and steadied him. The once-strong PAVN soldier was too dumbfounded to speak. His mind went blank over what the young officer from the Ministry in Hanoi had just shown him.

One thing was certain: the young officer had never been where Nghia had. Never fought in a deep jungle far from home. Nghi hadn't been wounded like he had. Hadn't seen death, tragedy, or destruction on that scale. And because of that, Nghia's mind went blank.

Nghia had been in the garden. A peaceful task—therapeutic, even. For most people. But he wasn't most people. He was a veteran of two wars. He'd spent years in the military, serving his country. First, fighting the French, then the Americans. He wasn't afraid of anything or anyone.

But just the sight of a copy of his old identification card gave him the shakes. His mind overloaded. After a few brief moments of silent processing, he found himself back in Kontum.

It was March 1968, and his memories closed in like a vice, squeezing the air thin. Fear pressed hard, loss gnawed deep, pain hung heavy like smoke that wouldn't clear. There was no stepping out of it, no safe distance—only the crushing weight of a moment that refused to die. He thought he'd let the past be the past long ago, but—at the sight of his papers—the war was back, raw, merciless, and inescapable.

Worse, he knew that was where he had lost his most treasured possession, the memory book. Vu's gift. The only piece of her he carried. Gone. Ripped from him like flesh torn open, another wound that would never close.

And after twenty-five years, crashed through his mind in an instant—he finally spoke.

"Yes. It is mine. That's me. Where did you get that?"

"We received the documents from an American, Mr. Steve Smith, the owner of a documentary film company. He asked the

Ministry of Foreign Affairs to help locate your family. And now that I'm certain I have the correct Nguyen Van Nghia... there's something else I need to tell you. There's another American, his name is Mr. Paul Reed. He's asked to meet your family—because he believes you died in battle at Kontum on March 17, 1968."

Luong Thanh Nghi continued, "Quite frankly, we informed Mr. Smith that we did not have information that you survived the war. And according to Mr. Paul Reed, he also believed you died in the war. That's the reason we have come here—to discover the truth."

"That's the same thing the Army told my wife in 1968," Nghia told the young officer, his words faltering. The weight of it left him reeling—confused, overwhelmed, unable to believe and accept what he was hearing.

Nghia hadn't a clue who these Americans—Steve Smith and Paul Reed—were, but after a long and serious look at the papers, he was convinced the papers were his.

The images on the papers were photocopies of his little memory book, which was lost in Kontum. There were pages and pages of poetry he'd written on the Truong Son range and during some of his darkest moments on the battlefield. Seeing the poetry he hadn't laid eyes on in years pulled the war into sharp focus again—the very war he had tried to forget. And as he read a few lines, the idea that the things he lost in battle might return after all these years struck him as nothing less than a miracle.

"But how can this be?" he asked.

That was when Nghi came back around to Mr. Smith.

"As I was saying earlier, the Ministry of Foreign Affairs was contacted by American Steve Smith regarding a film project. He has provided us with the proposal for a film to be made for American TV, and the Ministry has granted him permission.

"You understand that our two countries, America and Vietnam, do not have diplomatic relations at this time. Because of that, this project was very difficult to get approved. But the film's subject matter made it possible. That's why I have come to you today—to tell you the good news that the American will be returning everything he collected from your backpack during the war."

"Everything…?" Nghia asked, shrugging his shoulders.

Nghi replied, "That's what I understand."

"The subject matter of the film—what will it be?" Nghia asked.

"Good question—I'm glad you asked. Mr. Smith and his film crew will be escorting another American I mentioned earlier, Mr. Paul Reed. They'll be filming as Paul meets your wife face-to-face and returns to her the things he had taken from your backpack at Kontum.

"Please remember, Mr. Reed believes you died during the battle in Kontum, and Mr. Smith has accepted his belief as truth. But if you are found alive, that will mean a very big surprise—one they never thought possible.

"Mr. Smith has plans to escort Mr. Reed to the battlefield where you two first met in battle, and that's part of the film. But I can tell you now that once they find out you are alive, they will certainly ask you to go with them."

Nghia said nothing. The words reached him—but did not settle. Not yet. Kontum. The heat. The gunfire. The confusion. The men who never came back. And now… the American who had been there—who had taken his things… was coming back. Not in war. But in peace.

To stand before him. To return what had been lost. And possibly… to walk again on the same ground where they had once tried to kill each other. A weight rose inside him—part fear, part memory, part something he could not yet name. He thought of his comrades. Those who had suffered. Those who had died. What would this mean to them? What would it mean for him to stand beside a former enemy… in full view of others? The past he had carried quietly for so many years was no longer behind him. It was standing in front of him. Waiting.

What Nghia was hearing took a while to sink in.

Suddenly, Nghia spoke up, "My things—the American collected—does that mean my little book too? Is it coming back?"

"To the best of my knowledge and according to Mr. Steve Smith, that is correct."

For a moment, Nghia said nothing. The little book. The one Vu had placed in his hands before he left. The one he had carried through the jungle… through fear… through war. The one that held his thoughts when no one else could hear them.

He had believed it was lost forever—left somewhere on a battlefield where so much else had been left behind. But now—it was coming back. Not just to him—to her.

To the one who had given it to him—who had waited—who had believed he might one day return.

What would it mean for Vu to hold it again? To see his words… written in those days when death was never far away? To touch something that had traveled through war… and somehow found its way home?

There were many things going through Nghia's head as Nghi continued, "The American, Mr. Paul Reed, will be here to meet your wife in a few months."

As Nghi turned to leave, he said, "Don't forget, he believes you died back in 1968, during a mortar attack. Now that we have found you alive, he is in for a big surprise."

Soon after Nghi left, a panoramic full-view movie of his time in Kontum once again came into Nghia's sight, and it was as though he couldn't get it to stop this time.

Finally, the film in his head stopped, and he was able to focus on the present day, which left him with questions: "Was this Paul Reed part of the 173rd Airborne? And if so, was he one of the Americans who got my backpack?"

The sun was down, and darkness was about to descend on the village when Vu made it home. She climbed the stairs to their front door and began removing her shoes when Nghia called out to her.

He said softly, "Vu, Vu… do you remember? You gave me a small book before I went south to fight the Americans. I named it *Memories.*"

On the way to the oven, she laughed and said, "Yes, of course. Why?"

"Today, while you worked, an officer from the Ministry of Foreign Affairs paid us—well, me—a visit. He showed me papers and pages from the inside of that little book. Pages I myself wrote. He called them 'photocopies'...whatever that is."

She had been facing the oven, but when she heard what he'd just said, she turned to face him. "What did you tell him?" she asked.

I told him, "That's amazing. The small book has been gone for more than twenty-five years, which you had given me before the war took it away from me. I never believed I would see it again.

"He showed me the complete little book with my thoughts, memories, and poetry. Oh, so many thoughts and poems! When I asked where he got all my papers and the little book I called *Memories*, he told me an American man had them. They've been in America all this time, for the past twenty-five years—and they will soon come back to Vietnam, to us."

Vu brushed aside her husband's story as nothing more than another dream. Since he'd come home, he had been haunted by illusions and nightmares, and she had learned not to trust them. She responded, *"America is a long way from Vietnam. Your book of memories is lost forever."*

In her mind, no American would ever come to see them. Nghia's dreams since returning had already caused the family great turbulence, and she wasn't ready to accept this one as truth. But inside, she was thinking, "Could it be possible?"

He had seen that look before—the quiet dismissal, the need to protect herself from hope that might not be real. But inside, his thoughts did not leave him—the little book. He could still see it in her hands—the day she gave it to him. The way she had looked at him, not knowing if she would ever see him again. What would it mean for her to hold it once more? To open those pages. To see his handwriting. To read the words he had written in the middle of the jungle, when she was never far from his thoughts? To know that something from that time. Something of him—had survived?

He imagined her fingers tracing the worn edges, pausing over the lines he had written, perhaps seeing parts of him she had never known. Not the soldier. Not the war—but the man who had carried her with him—through it all.

He did not try to convince her. He only held onto the thought—quietly. That somehow what had been lost—might find its way back home.

Several weeks later, Luong Thanh Nghi showed up again. But this time, he was not alone. With him was Steve Smith. He came specifically to meet and interview Nguyen Van Nghia and Vu Thi Gai, his wife.

After their arrival, Vu believed her husband's story was not a dream.

Nghi told them that he would be Steve's translator. Steve introduced himself, "Ah, hello, I'm Steve Smith. It's nice meeting you both. Vu, I have a few questions just for you. I must verify the handwriting on the items we believe were written by your husband."

Steve reached into his backpack to retrieve the photocopies of Nguyen Van Nghia's complete writings and passed them to Vu.

After a moment of anxious silence and smiles, Steve asked, "Do you recognize the handwriting?"

She indicated she did.

"Whose handwriting is it?" Steve asked.

"That's my husband's handwriting."

"Okay. My next question is more of an affirmation. Please take your time. Can you point out something that would confirm the validity of what you just said—that the handwriting you are holding in your hands is your husband's?"

She flipped through the pages, pausing a few times. Then—pointing while nodding up and down—she said, "I've shown him the correct grammar many times, but these are his bad habits. Here, here, and here."

Steve and Nghi deemed the documents to be official.

Luong Thanh Nghi had located the actual author of the little book labeled *Memories,* and Steve breathed a sigh of relief as Vu passed the photocopies back to him.

The filmmaker in Steve thanked Nghi repeatedly, but the young officer acted as if it were no big deal.

"Finding him was easy," he said. "Vietnamese people generally are born, grow up, work and die in the same village."

Be that as it may, Steve was still grateful to the young officer who found the correct man. That meant—without a doubt—the man sitting before them, Mr. Nguyen Van Nghia, was in Kontum on March 17, 1968.

The two men had experienced enough excitement for the day and returned to Hanoi.

Over dinner that night, Vu and Nghia sat across from one another in silence.

That's not to say their minds weren't reflecting on what they had experienced earlier. Getting the visit from the American and the Foreign Affairs officer seemed like a good thing, but Nghia wasn't exactly sure. The war had been over for him twenty-five years. The kids had grown up. They'd reached a comfort level on par with most Vietnamese families. But neither he nor she understood why the past wasn't really the past—as they had often told themselves.

Nghia wondered to himself, *Why is this happening now? Why are the painful memories of long ago coming back? That was the past. Let the past be the past.*

He broke the silence.

"Vu… that little journal you gave me… I've been thinking about it."

She looked at him, softer now. "I could never forget that little book."

I bought it and gave it to you before you left for the south.

You were a poet. You love to write poetry. That's why I gave it to you. I told you when you filled its pages with the poetry of me, of us, I would always be by your side. As you read them, you would feel me there with you.

"Husband, besides the part about being by your side, I also had a strong belief about the book, and I told you that. Do you remember?"

"Yes, I do. You said both I and the memory-keeper would come back—that we would return to you. But how did you know?"

"Call it a woman's intuition or confidence. But my parents taught me—if I believe in something—to stand on it, and I have. I never really let go of my belief that both of you would return to me.

"Nearly twenty-five years ago, the military found me at work in the field. They said they were sorry, but they brought bad news. They told me that you died fighting the Americans in Kontum. Other women in the district had similar visits, so I knew what they would say. At first, I started to cry, but after a few moments, I stopped. I remembered my belief and told them you were not dead. They looked at me strangely when I asked them to show me the body of my husband. If they could do that, then I'd believe you were dead. But until then, I said I'd keep believing. They offered nothing more and then left.

"It seems like the night I said those things was only yesterday.

"My mother, seeing my suffering and difficulty as a single mother, tried to convince me to forget you and move on. But I still believed you would return to me. My fellow workers said I should forget you and move on, but I still believed.

"While American bombs burst near our village, and our children and I squatted in bomb shelters, shaking, scared we would soon die, I still believed. Playing your favorite flute melody every day as the sun came up—I believed you'd hear and return.

"Many—no, thousands and thousands of PAVN soldiers went south and never returned to their families in the north. But I never stopped believing what I told you then would come true. Every time I opened the newspapers and read about the fighting in the south, I held to my belief that you would return… and with you, the little volume you named *Memories*.

"Our hearts are connected. We are like two people, with only one heart. Separated for a time by our country, yes, but only temporarily. I believed our country would also reunite us one day.

"Not for a second did I believe you died. I believed one day you'd return. That is why I played the flute every day. I always believed."

And as his mind turned over the years, he thought about how fortunate he was to have her not only in his life, but as his wife.

Her love broke through when she added, *"Husband, love brought you home. And now love will bring the little book home—at the time it was meant to come."*

CHAPTER FIFTEEN

FIRST GOODWILL AMBASSADOR

On November 10, 1993, Steve, Phil Sturholm, Mike James, soundman Mark Waszkiewicz, and I circled Noi Bai Airport in a Thai Airlines jet.

The plane dropped its landing gear. Out the window, we could already see scars from the war—massive craters from B-52 strikes. Some held water like swimming pools. Others just stared back—open wounds on the land.

Hanoi was the city of my nightmares. The capital of the enemy. A place I'd been trained to hate without ever having seen it. And now, here I was.

As the plane touched down, I felt it. The old heat. The weight in my chest. All around the runway sat reminders: Russian MiGs, radar towers, and communication buildings. Former targets, that's what they were. I felt like I'd slipped into the past—back on some covert mission.

The antennas sent me straight over the edge. Hanoi Hannah was what we called her. She was the voice of North Vietnam, which floated into our personal AM/FM radios and through our earpieces at night, spitting out venom designed to demoralize us.

I remembered her voice, "You are finished. Jody—back home, stealing your girls. Today you die." Sometimes she was right, but when she wasn't, we fought harder. Just to shove it back in her face.

The plane stopped. The others stood up, calm and ready to disembark. I stayed seated. I looked left, then right, pretending to be a tourist. But I was frozen. I knew exactly who I was—Paul Reed, veteran, civilian, father, trucker, ex-husband. But if I stepped off that plane, I wasn't sure who I'd be.

That cabin was my shelter. My last link to the present. Stepping off meant war. No buffer. No warning. No easing my way back in. The moment my boots were to hit the ground, it was there—war, waiting, hungry. One step, and I would be swallowed whole.

A flight attendant touched my shoulder. "Sir, you'll have to exit now."

I stood slowly, grabbed my bag and camera, and walked the aisle like it was a tunnel back in the bush.

Outside, it was hot. Bright. Still.

Twenty-five years earlier, mortars, fighter jets, and B-52's had frequented these skies. Tet had just hit. The war still burned. Now—no rockets, no cordite, no M-60s, no AK-47s, no grenades, and no screaming. No fish sauce or gunpowder in the air. There was only silence.

I was walking into that silence. I went through customs. The bureaucrats were young—kids, really—barely out of diapers when their fathers were trying to kill my friends and me.

I thought to myself, *If these are the faces of my former enemies, they are a generation removed.*

Their eyes didn't hold hate. Their hands carried no blood. They felt like a cleansing wind, nature's way of healing the land—like flowers forcing their way up through soil once drenched in blood on the killing fields of Vietnam.

I glanced at the men on duty—two North Vietnamese, officials maybe, standing there unarmed. They were smiling. Relaxed. Their posture was easy, no edge in their eyes. No hidden signals. No danger. Just two men who actually seemed glad to see me.

The first Vietnamese to speak to me introduced himself as **Luong Thanh Nghi,** from the Ministry of Foreign Affairs. He was twenty-nine, handsome, spoke flawless English, and from that moment on would be my translator.

The second man, much older, was **Nguyen Van Nghi**—my driver and guide. Like me, he was a veteran. He had fought in the war against France, the one they won at Dien Bien Phu. He carried himself with pride for his service and the honor he earned through heroism.

Nguyen's government job as a guide was proof that his country still respected him. At one point, he pulled out a photograph—him and a friend in uniform, standing shoulder to shoulder during their war. And looking at him, I couldn't help but see myself—another soldier, another war, another time.

A day or two earlier in the U.S., Steve Smith had informed me that the man I believed had died during our battle at Kontum was actually alive—and wanted to meet me—so it would be no surprise if I heard it again once I landed in Hanoi. Nonetheless, a young man from the Ministry of Foreign Affairs, Mr Luong Thanh Nghi, my translator for the entire trip, out of courtesy, broke the same news to me I'd learned from Steve earlier—Nghia was alive—and was looking forward to our meeting.

"Have you met Mr. Nguyen Van Nghia?" I asked, curious as to what kind of reception I'd receive. "Does he know I'm coming? What kind of person is he? Does he want to meet me?"

Nghi smiled and said, "Yes, I've met him. He knows you're coming, and he's expecting you. He's a veteran of the French and American wars. A very nice gentleman."

His comment startled me. I wrongly assumed that Nghia and I were contemporaries. I had figured him to be in his late forties or early fifties.

"Is he older than me? How much older?"

"I think he's about sixty-five," Nghi said, with an inquiring look on his face.

I was startled. The photograph, which I studied over and over, was of a much younger man. The idea that I might be a generation removed from my former enemy was something unexpected. It shouldn't have mattered—but it did. Confusion swept through me.

I pulled out the photograph I thought was Nghia and asked, *"You mean this isn't the man I've come to see?"*

Nghi looked at it curiously, as though wondering why it was in my hand. "That's right," he replied on the way to their car, "that's not him."

At the car, I was met with a courteous, humble gesture of respect. Nghi opened the door, motioned me inside, and said, *"Welcome, Mr. Ambassador."*

I froze. That title belonged to polished men in suits, backed by governments and official seals—not to truck drivers or broken-down grunts carrying ghosts. But I knew what he meant. I told him I wasn't an ambassador.

"Oh, but you are, sir," he replied. *"You are our first American goodwill ambassador since the war ended."*

Paul Reed with Luong Thanh Nghi, Hanoi, 2018.
Twenty-five years after he first said,
"Welcome, Mr. Ambassador."

That night, the film crew and I went to the Piano Restaurant and Bar on Hang Vai Street for dinner. The restaurant specialized in Vietnamese and Chinese cuisines, and I delighted in authentic fried rice. The eatery was more sophisticated than I expected, and many people had incomes adequate to enjoy it, but the old ways were still acceptable.

It was late when we finished our dinner, and the hotel was far enough from the restaurant, so we decided to hail a cyclo-driver. This was a type of rickshaw powered by a solo driver. Competition among the men who operated them was fierce, and the effort to hail one brought fifteen drivers instantly vying for our business.

The cyclo-drivers rode with the same reckless abandon as New York cabbies. In Hanoi, there were only a handful of traffic lights—

and collisions were common. A ride could turn wild in an instant as drivers weaved and lunged, fighting for inches on the crowded backstreets. Locals braced for it, but tourists were the only ones spared from the daily grind of vehicles pressing too close.

The drivers rang a handlebar-mounted bell every few feet, a signal that the passenger was a foreigner. The sound made people step back, giving the cyclo more space. It was their way of smoothing the ride for tourists—an effort, it seemed, to make sure the foreigners came back.

Peddlers were everywhere, hawking their wares. It took me right back to South Vietnam, where every price was at least double—either to haggle down and still turn a profit, or to soak the foreigners who didn't know better. Nothing had changed—I learned quickly when I picked up an English/Vietnamese phrasebook. The asking price was two dollars, but the real price was only one dollar. I bought it anyway, shaking my head, amused that some games in Vietnam never died.

I wasn't reliving the jungle. I knew where I was—in Hanoi. But I couldn't adjust to the truth that the war was over, that a tall American wasn't automatically a target. Not for a bullet. Not for a grenade. Not for a knife. The silence pressed in, and still the thought haunted that at any moment, the Viet Cong could slip out of the dark and be on top of me.

In the hotel, I slipped out of bed quietly, the old jungle instincts rising as if my last ambush had been only yesterday. It struck me how easily they came back—how quickly my body remembered, even when my mind tried to forget after all these years. I scanned the room, listening hard, every nerve awake, every sense sharpened. Slowly, I moved to the balcony door. It was still shut. Still locked. No one had touched it. Yet part of me knew I would always be checking, always expecting shadows.

Slowly, I opened the door and stepped onto the balcony. My eyes swept the darkness, searching for the places an attack might come from. Everything was still. Peaceful. The only weight was the humidity—so heavy it pressed down like a storm about to break. I stood in the shadows, silent, listening for minutes that felt longer. No movement. No enemy. No rattle of AKs. No thump of mortars. And yet the restlessness stayed. Calm didn't come until nearly an hour later.

I wrote in my journal, watched a lizard inch up the wall, and tried to settle myself. Exhaustion finally won, and I slept for a couple of hours. The sound of soft chimes woke me. I ran to the window, then checked the clock; it was 6 a.m., and daylight was just breaking, Hanoi already alive. A fierce game of badminton in the street. The noise of people heading to work. I wanted to be up too, and since I couldn't eat in my room as planned, I went down to the hotel restaurant for bananas, papaya, orange juice, and toast.

Steve Smith and the crew—Phil Sturholm, Mike James, and Mark Waszkiewicz—were already there. Not long after, Nghi joined us to map out the day's trip to Thai Binh and to tell us about Nguyen Van Nghia.

In 1965, when the American War intensified, loudspeakers called for troops to fight in the South. Nghia's wife and children urged him to rejoin the army. He was thirty-seven—a veteran already of the French war. They knew what it could cost him, but they felt he had to do something for the nation.

His family received a small sum when he went back to duty. They dreamed of time together, but it never came. The war was too fierce. He was too far from home. And the few areas set aside for rest were dangerous—American patrols in the south made travel impossible. He wrote to his wife often, but only one letter ever reached her after several years.

At home, his wife became both mother and father, raising crops, making money, and caring for the children in his absence. It was the same story for countless women in North Vietnam—just as in the United States during World War II, where women stepped into roles men had left behind. Independence changed them.

Nghia's family, his wife and children, still deferred to him—his service and sacrifice commanded their respect, even though his wounds left him unable to work the land again once he returned home.

What I didn't realize was that Nghia didn't share my emotions about meeting former enemies. He wasn't bitter. He wasn't angry. His beliefs were rooted in the ancients—the past—whether yesterday or decades ago—was over. It held no meaning. Only the present and the future mattered.

"The moment Nghia left the battlefield," Nghi said, "Mr. Reed, you were no longer his enemy."

The words settled into me slowly. I had crossed an ocean carrying a war that had ended decades ago, while the man I came to face had already laid it down. He had walked away from the battlefield, and I had carried it home.

Standing there in Hanoi, I began to understand something I had only glimpsed before. War could scar the land. It could take youth, years, friends, and sleep. It could teach men to hate and call it duty, but it could not reach or destroy everything.

It could not kill what still lived beneath the uniform. It could not erase what waited inside a man once the guns went silent. And it could not keep two former enemies from becoming human again.

Nghi paused. "The war ended, and with it the anger, the hatred, the desire for revenge. Nghia understood that what was right in times of violence was not right in times of peace. He neither hates nor fears you, Mr. Reed. The shooting stopped, and for twenty-five years since, you—once his enemy—were already his friend."

Nghi looked across the table at me and smiled, softer this time.

"Perhaps we were right to call you Mr. Ambassador. You have carried more than a diary across the years—you have carried the seeds of reconciliation. In returning it, you have become a personal bridge between two former enemies. And perhaps one day, the bridge you began here now will not end with two men, or even two families, but will help bring healing and reconciliation between two nations still scarred by war. And when that day comes, let history remember that it all began when you both were called—and answered the call—to serve your nations."

Only half of us at the table were veterans. But when Nghi finished speaking, every one of us was ready to meet the man—the poet, the uncle, the battlefield warrior—all made possible because of the little fake alligator-skin book that had a voice, and it spoke.

The little journal had traveled full circle around the earth—through the air, across the seas—and was returning to its rightful owner. Not by pact. Not by fairness. Not even by justice. But because something greater was at work—love—and love brought it home.

CHAPTER SIXTEEN

ONCE AN ENEMY

When we reached the Red River on the way to Mr. Nghia's house, the driver told us we'd have about a forty-five–minute wait. The bridge across the river had been bombed during the war, and the only way over now was by ferry.

Once the ferry carried our vehicle across and we were back on the road, the film crew broke into laughter. Sturholm cracked a joke that they ought to build a new bridge and name it the *Nguyen Van Nghia and Paul Reed Memorial Bridge.*

The laughter helped. It broke through the knot of tension building in me—about where I was headed and how I'd be received.

The drive to Thai Binh City, the capital of Thai Binh Province, where Nghia lived, took 3.5 hours from Hanoi. By the time we arrived, fear was riding close. His home sat off what looked like a narrow alley—a two-story building on the right, and a one-story on the left. The right side was for business, the lower floor for the shop or trade, and the upper for living quarters.

The alley itself was just wide enough for a van. Dense vegetation blocked the view down a smaller path branching off the main lane, where the interpreter told the driver to stop. The thick foliage pulled me straight back to places where my men and I once set up ambushes. In combat, you never trusted a trail. The reality of a sniper's bullet waited.

"Are you ready?" Nghi asked.

I didn't know if I was. But I nodded like I was.

A cluster of children had gathered, watching me silently. Maybe they wondered why two cameras followed my every move. Maybe they just wondered if I was really that different. I found myself asking the same thing. Later, I learned they had never seen an American before.

Privately, I thought about turning back. Running. Grabbing a weapon. Or slipping away. As we closed those last steps, a wild thought crossed my mind—asking if Nghia had any AK-47s or grenades stashed away. But that thought fell off quickly when I remembered my welcome at Noi Bai Airport.

And then we rounded the corner.

Nghia stood in his courtyard,—green shirt, and darker green pants. His family stood close to the house, lined up behind him, watching from a distance—almost as frightened of me as I was of them.

When we came face to face, Nghia was visibly shaken. His hands trembled—like a young boy afraid of something he didn't understand. But I didn't feel fear. Something else came over me. In an instant, I was back in Kontum—standing in the jungle, flipping through the small book I had taken from his backpack. And then it hit me—this was not our first meeting. We had met years before.

Two lives—one North Vietnamese, one Western American—set in motion by different voices, different worlds, somehow drawn across oceans, across war, across everything meant to divide us—into the same country, the same battle, the same moment—both of us trying to kill the other. Looking back, it no longer felt like coincidence. It felt as though something had been tracing a line between us all along, long before we ever saw it, long before we ever walked it.

In a way I could not fully explain all those divisions, but they were obvious when we fired on one another during the war. And this moment—standing face to face in his courtyard—was the completion of that mindset.

This day had been a long time coming. Two former battlefield enemies who once desired nothing more than the other's demise looked deeply into each other's eyes as Smith, Sturholm, and the sound man, Waszkiewicz, zoomed in, making sure they captured everything on film.

I was a big American, much larger than him, my hands capable of engulfing his, when suddenly he placed both my hands in his own. He held them the way a father might hold those of a child sitting up in bed, afraid of whatever lurks in the darkness. The older man was at once loving and reassuring, saying more with a touch and a look than I could express in words.

I noticed only gentleness and a degree of jitters—Nghia's knees were shaking. I wasn't without my own nervousness and mistakenly addressed Nghia by calling him our translator Nghi's given name, Nghi, since they were so similar. Smith always said I should give up trying to speak their language, because it always came out wrong and they wound up laughing.

Nghi ignored the mistake and simply translated. "How do you do?"

My thoughts ever since I knew Nghia was alive had been about what to say once I learned he was alive, but suddenly I went silent. Everything seemed so awkward—until Nghia's reply.

Nghia answered the question posed to him in Vietnamese, which, translated to English, meant, *"I'm fine, thank you. Won't you join me for tea?"*

Then, taking me by the hand, he gently led me into his house and offered me a place to sit at their dining table. The front doors and windows were wide open, as they usually were, due to the normal temperature, and the light was comforting.

The invitation to tea was customary—a ritual of politeness. And when we entered the home, small by American standards but quite comfortable for Nghia and his family, there were several people sitting on a rice mat bed at one end of the room. I did not know if they were family members, neighbors, or others who had come to see the American. Certainly, there was more company than I expected, for every place to sit was taken—small chairs, the windowsill, even each other's laps. All were smiling. All seemed genuinely glad to see the man who'd come so far to meet one of their own.

Children from the neighborhood peered in through open windows. The house was a comfortable size, 20 × 20, raised up two steps, and clad in faded yellow stucco. Open shutters would keep out bad weather when closed. Inside, the walls were decorated with colorful posters, and curtains could be pulled for privacy. Besides the large bed, there were several chairs, one small table, and one large table. The kitchen was in the corner, diagonally from the bed.

There was running water, yet the family toilet was outside, around the corner—reminding me of a farmer's house where I got sick during the war. Electricity was limited to one five-watt bulb hanging from the ceiling.

The very best china was being used; eight teacups on eight saucers had been arranged around the table.

Still frightened of the unknown, I hoped to sit on the chair placed closest to the door. I wanted to be able to flee, to leave the house, and leave the country if necessary. Nghia would have nothing to do with my wishes, though. It was important that I showed deference for Nghia's wife—the woman Nghia loved and to whom so much of his writing was dedicated—and the son who let him retain his pride. Nghia sat on my left, his wife on the right. He was honoring her, and my fears would have to be ignored in light of that.

The conversation briefly turned to my family—again, a ritual. I was then supposed to ask about Mr. Nghia's. Although I was coached on this ritual, I forgot it when I arrived. Although I failed to ask Nghia about his own family, he ignored the mistake. Such manners seemed of minor consequence given the importance of the moment.

We sat together, hands folded in our respective laps, our bodies tense. There was no anger, no hint of hostility. Rather, it was the nervousness of a blind date—of courtship without knowledge of the other person. Finally, Nghia tried to become more personal.

"I am very moved and very pleased to have you here in my home," said Nghia. "It is quite a long trip to Vietnam. You got my pack during the war. Now you bring it to my home. I am so very happy."

As I spoke, hesitantly at first, then more comfortable about telling the story of mailing everything I'd taken from the man's backpack—home—where it sat in an attic for more than twenty years—I glanced at Nghia's wife. She sat on my right, acting as though we were long-time friends. She made me feel at home, having none of the hesitancy, nervousness, or reservations apparent in her husband.

Doesn't she know who she's sitting next to? I wondered to myself. Does she understand I was the enemy Nghia fought in the south?

Yet she was the one to whom I once believed I would be delivering Nghia's things to including the little book that held words reaching far beyond war. Until recently, I ponderously thought of myself as the soldier who had robbed her of a husband and father of their children. How it turned out differently, I wasn't sure. But I was happy that Nghia, the poet, hadn't died at my hand and was alive, albeit visibly weak and wounded.

In my fantasies of soldiers from the north, they appeared invincible on the battlefield—almost untouchable—there was nothing they could not achieve. Yet here was a man who was physically and emotionally shattered, at least as much as, if not more than, me. The pain we both bore through our experience was the price of war.

Suddenly, there was clarity in the moment. As with her husband, the past was always over and must not color the present. Had I killed her husband during the war, the act of returning his things would have resulted in the same warm, friendly greeting. She was as sensitive to life as her poet-soldier husband. The hate-filled anger that had so thoroughly consumed me during the last decades was incomprehensible to this couple.

Just as the war had to be fought as savagely as necessary to win, so the peace had to be lived with enduring gentleness, love, and respect for the former enemy.

Nghia's daughter and two of his three sons, along with a daughter-in-law, son-in-law, and grandchild, were there. The other people were friends. It was an important time for them—a chance to meet an American who had faced their father during one of Vietnam's many wars.

They knew who I was, my calling from the past. But they cared more about who I was today. They were delighted to meet me, to enjoy my company. I was the first American ever to visit their village.

The atmosphere was like being newly married and having dinner at an in-law's house, where everyone knows you, likes you, and wants you to be comfortable. Mrs. Nghia poured the tea, and I practiced my limited knowledge of Vietnamese, against Smith's recommendation.

I was in shock. I was having tea with a former PAVN enemy soldier. Many of my fellow patriots would simply pass out if they could see this. Yet I, too, had hated this man—hated his family, his beliefs, everything about him, even his country. Now things were different. I liked—even loved—him, realizing I respected him more than many Americans I knew.

Nghia had answered his call. It was something I could relate to and understand.

The talk and the tea ritual continued. Then, before it was time to exchange the old possessions, there was one last rite to perform. Nghia brought out his finest rice liquor. I didn't drink much anymore. After all the traumas in my life, I'd learned liquor didn't really agree with me. Still, I knew it would be an insult not to share a drink with the man, so I took a glass.

Nghia filled our teacups, and we toasted, pretending to savor the moment. I lifted mine, sniffed, and immediately realized it was strong. I hesitated, watching him down it in one gulp. Then he turned to me with a small, expectant smile—as if to say, *No more stalling—bottoms up.*

The liquor burned like fire going down, searing my throat, nose, and the roof of my mouth. I coughed twice, tried to cover it with a smile, and croaked out in a weird sounding voice, "Excellent." My eyes watered, and I turned my head, hoping anyone who noticed would mistake it for emotion… not the drink. But maybe it was both.

There we sat—two former enemies—sharing a drink in his home. Not in anger. Not in fear. But in something neither of us could have imagined all those years before.

I told him about reading his little book—and how it made me see that he and I were alike in many ways. I explained, as best I could, how deeply I had been touched by the parts he wrote about his wife.

In his small book of poems, he had written that his sons looked like him and his daughter looked like his wife. Sitting there in his home, I could see he had been right. When I mentioned it, the whole family burst into laughter. In that moment, the distance between us—years, war, language—seemed to fade.

I was able to verify what Vinh had said about him—Nghia was a good man.

I asked Nghia what he remembered about the war. Very little, he explained. The bombing by the B-52s had taken much of that from him. His left eye was blinded. His right eye saw little.

And yet, with some reluctance—I reached for the box. The same box that had carried everything I'd taken from his backpack to America. It had sat quietly for years—holding pieces of a life interrupted. And now—that aforementioned box was bringing them home. I opened it slowly.

One by one, began removing the items—placing them carefully in front of Nghia. He leaned forward, his one good eye fixed on each piece as it emerged, as if trying to recognize something long buried in memory. Then it came—the little book. I paused.

For a moment, I just held it in my hands, while glancing at Nghia and Vu. Twenty-five years, I thought to myself.

Through war, through distance, through a life I never expected to live.

This small book had been there.

Not just a possession, but something that had changed me, something that had loosed the chains of hatred from my heart, and gave me reason to live.

Vu was already studying the small book in my hands closely. Quite. Still. As I slowly turned toward her, I extended the small book to her. She didn't reach for it right away, but her eyes stayed on it—taking it all in, as if needing to be certain what she was seeing was real. Then gently, she lifted her hands and received it.

She held it carefully, almost reverently, like something that had once been lost could disappear again if held too quickly. I watched her stroke the cover with her fingers. And then, she opened it, flipping the pages as if she were looking for something—for a moment there, I thought she was looking for some of the grammatical mistakes Nghia often made. We waited while she said nothing.

Then softly, she said, while looking at Nghia, "this is the same book I gave to you before you went south to fight," before glancing back down at the pages.

"I told you…"

Her fingers rested on the paper.

"…that you would come back."

She paused.

"And the little book…"

She lifted it slightly, as if to show it—

"…would come back too."

Not a soul moved. No one spoke. So quiet, a pin hitting the floor could be heard.

With bated breath, everyone watched her turn another page.

Suddenly she stopped again.

We watched her trace the words with her finger—reading what her husband had written about her all those years ago.

I glanced at Nghia. A slow grin spread across his face—one that seemed to carry both relief and something deeper. She had finally seen what he had carried for her all those years.

Not as her memory would have, but as something alive again, like, something returned. Nghia's eyed were fixed on her. Not the book—on her.

And in that moment, I understood—this was never about returning what had been taken. It was about restoring something that had never truly been lost.

Something that had endured, across war, across time, across everything meant to keep it from returning. And now, it was home.

For twenty-five years, the contents of that pack had been mine. More recently, when they were rediscovered, they had become part of my own healing—part of how I began to understand—and to help others understand. I had carried them from battlefield warrior—to something I never expected to become. And now, I was letting them go.

It was both bitter—and sweet. Bitter—because I was releasing something that had walked with me through my own transformation. Sweet—because it was never truly mine. It belonged to him. And to her.

His belongings—long thought lost—had somehow traveled across oceans, across years, across everything that should have kept them apart—and returned. He lifted his hand and twirled his finger in the air, smiling—tracing the journey they had made. I caught the gesture and nodded. A silent understanding passed between us. That even after war—after time—after distance—some things still come full circle.

And then I looked at Vu. Her expression was calm. Unshaken. Almost as if she had been expecting this moment all along. And then she spoke. She shared the dream she had carried for years—that both Nghia and the little book would return to her.

It was the first time I had heard it.

And the way she spoke—it did not feel like remembering a dream. It felt like revealing something she had always known. Not hoped. Known. As if, even after two and a half decades—this moment had never been in doubt.

The pictures—slightly embarrassing for Nghia but a delight to his children and friends. In wartime, it was common for friends to exchange small photographs when parting. I noticed one particularly beautiful young woman, whom Nghia explained was the sister of a friend. It was the only moment Mrs. Nghia seemed even slightly unsettled. She looked at the photos with tight lips, then looked away.

The pictures of other pretty girls brought laughter from his children, who enjoyed his obvious discomfort. Nghia tried to explain that it was common—pretty girls often gave passing soldiers their photos. He was as embarrassed as if the girls in the pictures were still young, though most were likely grandparents by now, just like him. He had clearly made peace with his former enemy—but not quite with the flirtations of a lonely soldier surviving in foreign territory. I was beginning to like Nghia a lot. In my heart, I knew where I was and what was happening. But in the back of my mind, doubt crept in—what if he wasn't the right man? He couldn't answer some of my questions about Kontum, and that unsettled me.

I showed him a picture inscribed with "Your loving sister," and Nghia couldn't identify the face. Something inside me buckled. Suddenly, I was convinced I'd been brought to the wrong man, the wrong family. *They're trying to deceive me. Maybe hurt me.* I didn't know what was happening—and that lack of control scared me.

"That's my southern sister," Nghia finally explained, as if that settled it. But I didn't understand what those words meant in Vietnamese culture. A southern sister wasn't family—it was a comrade, someone who shared your beliefs, your cause, your fight. It had nothing to do with intimacy. The meeting might have lasted just minutes—long enough to exchange a photo and a few words of support.

The doubt was too much. I jumped to my feet and asked Smith to meet me outside. "What's wrong?" he asked. "That's not the right Nghia in there," I said, my voice tight.

Smith didn't flinch. "Yes, it is. You don't know it, but we checked him out long before you came here. His wife confirmed the words written in his little book were her husband's. That man inside. We asked how she knew. She said, 'I always tried to teach him not to make mistakes.' Then she showed us the exact grammatical mistakes he still makes. That's how we knew. He's your man. That book placed him in Kontum."

When I went back inside, I remembered Nghia's old identification card from the pack—the one with his photo taken when he was young. The card listed several identifying marks, including a small black scar under the right side of his chin. I pulled it out and mentioned the scar. Dien, one of Nghia's sons, jumped up, walked over, and gently pointed beneath his father's chin—to the same scar.

I smiled. *This is my man,* I thought. The doubt was gone. We had the correct Nguyen Van Nghia.

Later, when I was calmer, I realized the doubts had come from me—because I expected too much. Access to after-action reports, letters, and maps gave me an advantage over raw remembrance. I'd studied the battle for years. Nghia only had his memory—and after what he had lived through, even that had faded. It wasn't fair to hold him to the same standard. He remembered what he could.

And then—there was the tiny journal—the instrument that had broken my hatred and set my heart free from a tormented life. As I reached into the box, I found myself whispering a silent prayer, *God, give me the strength to hand this over.*

Then I spoke aloud. "This small book helped me see you as a good person. Before I read it..." My eyes filled with tears. My face tightened. I spoke slowly, carefully, making sure Mr. Nghi would understand every word—so Nghia could hear what was really in my heart. "…I did not like you. You and your unit killed some of my friends."

As Nghi translated my words, Nghia looked straight into my face—calm, steady, almost as if he had understood long before today. His face was full of emotion, but not the kind I expected. There was no anger. No shame. Not even a trace of the terrible losses he had carried through the years—not even the fact that American soldiers, men like me, had killed his younger brother. Instead, there was something deeper—quiet strength mixed with a kind of grace, as if he had already made peace with all of it long before I ever walked into his courtyard. In his eyes, I saw not just a man who had survived, but a man who had forgiven.

Only the quiet weight of a man facing the truth that all soldiers eventually must—war doesn't leave anyone untouched.

As I continued, both cameras zoomed in, and Waszkiewicz, the sound man, stepped closer with the mic.

"I want you to know—I hated you. Deeply. But I know you lost friends, just like we did. And in your small book, you wrote that you were angry at me."

Nghia nodded gently, then smiled.

I looked at him and asked, "Are you still angry?"

I began to relax. The emotion of the moment had washed over me, but I knew—I needed peace. We were no longer enemies. We were comrades-in-arms who had worn different uniforms, came from different worlds, and fought on opposite sides—only because of where we'd been born.

"Do you forgive me—and my unit?" I asked.

He gestured by nodding his head up and down, indicating he understood my question.

Then he replied…

"Forget the past," Nghia said, smiling with me now. "Now we are friends. I'm grateful it's behind us. I'm very happy I lived to see this day."

There were no plans to ask that. The question came from somewhere deeper than thought.

Decades had passed—I refused to think about the people who had lost loved ones, homes, and their entire way of life. Refused to consider that the men of North Vietnam had paid a much steeper price than we had. Most of us—infantry troops—went home after a single year. For them, the war never really stopped.

I refused to face what most wars conceal—that when two sides are locked in conflict, there's your version, their version—and a truth somewhere in between.

I looked into Nghia's eyes, his emotions written all over his face. My trip had been driven by anger, by curiosity—by the need to see, face to face, the man whose memory had haunted me. Nghia had become the vessel for my demons—for the sleepless nights, the flashbacks, the broken pieces of my life that never quite fit.

And now I understood—I wasn't entirely right on things, or entirely wrong. We both carried the same weight. We both feared and resented each other—for the same reasons.

The little book—tucked away for years in a box in an attic—had not simply waited—it had been arranging our steps all along. From our callings to our battles, to our years of separation, and now to this meeting. A small book, fragile in form, yet powerful enough to bind our stories together long before we knew what was being written.

And between the two of us, it was the older man who had reached that truth first—that there are some things war cannot destroy!

CHAPTER SEVENTEEN

THEY MIRRORED ONE ANOTHER

To have the poetry he wrote—along with the rest of his belongings—returned by an American did more than surprise Nghia. It validated him. It validated his service, his sacrifice, and the years he had given to a cause that had nearly cost him his life. No one—not even his family—could truly step into the jungle he had walked, or feel the weight he had carried on the Truong Son trail. They loved him, yes. But they could not mirror him. Yet here I was—a former enemy who had crossed an ocean to find him.

In that moment, Nghia was no longer just a retired veteran in Thai Binh. He was once again the officer who had led men into battle. He was seen. Understood. All reflected back to himself, and something changed.

That one act—returning a small diary—elevated him. Maybe not for the first time in his life, but certainly for the first time in twenty-five years. It restored something war had taken. He was no longer only the assumed head of his household because of age or tradition. He stood again as the man who had earned that place.

If I were to guess, Nghia felt that elevation in more ways than one. Not long after our meeting, I learned his military pension had doubled, which stopped me cold. For decades, he had carried wounds no one could see. For decades, he had lived quietly—respected in his village, yes—but largely unseen by the larger machinery that once sent him south.

Then, suddenly, after an American veteran returned his belongings from two and a half decades earlier, something almost unthinkable in his world happened—as the cameras began documenting his life story as a combat officer and survivor, his standing shifted.

In a culture where recognition flows from the state downward, not from former enemies across oceans, what happened next was rare. His pension increased. Was it a coincidence? Perhaps. But to me, it felt like acknowledgment.

- Acknowledgment that he had been there.
- Acknowledgment that he had bled.
- Acknowledgment that he had nearly lost a leg along with other near-fatal wounds that should have ended his life—but didn't.
- Acknowledgment that his story mattered.

For twenty-five years, he had simply endured. Now he was seen. And that mattered. War had once defined him by the enemy he fought. Now, history was beginning to define him by the man he was.

In that restoration, I saw something powerful—when we choose to honor even those we once fought against, dignity rises on both sides.

The next item I pulled from the box was the Viet Cong flag, commonly known as the NLF (National Liberation Front) flag, which had been taken from Nghia's backpack.

Vietcong flag Nghia had in his backpack.

The one I gave him was actually a replica made by a seamstress in Hanoi. It was intended to substitute for the real one I handed Captain Davis that scorching hot, humid day in Kontum—while searching Nghia's backpack. Still, the meaning was the same. It had been many years since Nghia had seen such a flag.

The flag had been used only in the South, and while possession of one is still legal today, displaying it on a flagpole is not. By the time I finished explaining the excitement of capturing Nghia's backpack in the jungle, of opening it and finding the flag, Nghia draped it over his arm. With genuine excitement, he began explaining the meaning of the colors and the star.

"There is red on top, blue on the bottom, and a bright yellow star in the middle," he said, pointing to each part. The red stood for a unified country, the yellow star represented all the "bright, shining people." In Vietnam, blue signifies a sad spirit, so placing blue at the bottom symbolized the South—cut off and separated since 1954.

According to Nghia, as early as 1940, Ho Chi Minh had designed the national flag—a solid red field with a yellow star in the middle. During the war, the NLF flag was used to represent southern sympathizers who supported the North's efforts to reunify the nation.

Finally, and now emotionally drained, I gave Smith the nod—it was my signal that all of Nghia's items had been returned. Smith gave me a thumbs-up and a smile, as if to say, "Good job, I'm proud of you."

Nghia, visibly overcome like the father of a newborn child, was choked up and could not speak. If his face said anything, it was that he held a deep gratitude inside—a gratitude he had likely never experienced before.

When he finally could speak, Nghi translated, "Everything you brought back means so much. But because the small book was given to me by Vu, it is my most favorite. Along the way, during some of my most inspirational moments, I recorded thoughts of love about my wife, my family, and my country. I do not discount the value of the other items, please understand, but of all you returned, my little poem book means the most.

"I was in the underground hospital, doctors told me they had to amputate my leg, when I asked them about my things in our diversionary camp. It was then I learned all of our things had been taken by the Americans. I remember that day like it was yesterday.

For years, I believed it was gone forever.

Now, standing there in his own home, he lifted the little book—for everyone to see—his hand trembling slightly. He looked at it for a long moment, seemingly trying to understand its long journey and how it found its way back to him, to them.

Then he spoke, slowly and carefully, saying he had no words. Only that, this was something he could not have imagined.

He lowered the book and glanced toward Vu, and from the look on his face, we could see there was more in his heart than gratitude. There was something much deeper. There was relief—as if a part of his life that had been left behind—had finally returned to him.

Truthfully, without the input from Dale Ducet of Louisiana, I might never have thought beyond returning Nghia's possessions. But the joy of the moment was overwhelming—not much different from the exuberance I felt each time my son knocked a home run for his baseball team.

I did not realize how honored I would feel, traveling there and meeting the man I once disrespected, the man whom, over the years, I had hated, a man I once believed my hand had killed but now cared for deeply. In that exact moment, I made a vow to myself: I would never again disrespect any Vietnamese person.

Lieutenant Nghia was a man—just as human as I was. There was no other explanation for the spirit of oneness that had overcome me after my mom read Nghia's poem titled "Love."

In a festive mood, Mrs. Nghia invited me to stay for lunch, which I gratefully accepted. I was seated facing the same door where we had met only moments earlier. When I glanced toward it, I was startled—though I shouldn't have been—by what hung above the frame: a nicely rendered portrait of Jesus Christ.

While pointing to the image, I glanced toward Nghia and smiled, expressing my pleasure at seeing a similar image hanging above the door of my father's bedroom.

The image wasn't ornate or extravagant. Just a simple depiction—gentle eyes, steady gaze, a face marked by both sorrow and peace. It hung above the entrance, positioned where every person entering or leaving the house would pass beneath it.

In Vietnam, ancestor altars are common. Portraits of Ho Chi Minh are common. But the image of Christ was something different. It told me something about the home I was sitting in. It told me this was a house shaped not only by war, not only by patriotism, not only by sacrifice—but by faith.

I couldn't help but think about the symbolism of its placement. Above the doorway. Above the threshold. Almost as if guarding what entered and exited. As if to say, "Whoever crosses this line must answer to something higher."

I thought about the years Nghia spent in the jungle. The wounds. The underground hospital. The two years his wife believed him dead. Their poverty. The quiet endurance. And now this moment—an American once sworn to destroy his country, sitting at his table, returning the last pieces of his humanity.

If reconciliation had a doorway, I realized, I had just walked through it. And above that doorway hung the face of the One who taught oneness, forgiveness, love, and that love bears no grudge.

Soon, the table was filled with bowls of rice, fresh vegetables, and steaming dishes full of meat. Nghia took the first step. He placed some meat in my bowl and smiled, inviting me to eat. Savoring the moment, I tried my hand at Vietnamese and asked for chopsticks.

Somehow, Vu Thi Gai understood. She repeated, "Mot doi dua, cam on yeu," and handed them to me, clearly delighted by the effort. Everyone laughed.

Later, I learned why. I requested chopsticks, but the way I pronounced it came out sounding like a very personal word for love. Vu's graciousness didn't allow for embarrassment. Instead, she responded with kindness—and laughter.

What struck me most was that my former enemy had just offered to feed me—an act of simple kindness, but one that carried amazing weight.

In many respects, the conversation with Nghia that afternoon confirmed the message I'd once received from God—back in Dallas, when raging at Him. My purpose, I learned, was to tell this story of reconciliation, forgiveness, and friendship for the rest of my life. Now it was clearer than ever. My calling—from the past—had been confirmed, and through, of all people, a former enemy.

Nghia took another look at the photographs but struggled to make them out. When asked how he lost sight in one eye and was partially blinded in the other, he explained that his eyes had been burned by the defoliant Agent Orange that the Americans sprayed from the air.

Shortly after the near-blinding incident, Nghia returned to his unit—and that was when our paths first crossed, unknowingly, during combat action on Hill 1064. Neither of us realized it at the time or distance, but we were there, facing each other's fire.

He explained how PAVN intelligence had operated much like the Americans. They tracked units, knew who they were up against, and followed us almost everywhere through the jungle. Helicopters were impossible to conceal—the sound gave us away. They heard them coming, heard the landings, heard us pushing through the underbrush.

With a mix of pride and humility, I asked Nghia what he thought when he learned that it wasn't the First Cavalry Division his unit was fighting, but the 173rd Airborne. He admitted it worried them. The 173rd had a fearsome reputation. Skilled fighters. Heavy artillery. Relentless air support. He'd heard the stories of Dak To, of Hill 875 in the Cherry Hill cluster, and he knew what kind of men we were.

When he finished, Nghia paused, then said quietly, "It was the roughest fighting I'd ever seen."

I thought he'd finished speaking when something came over him. Dropping his gaze to the floor, he calmly mentioned his younger brother dying in Kontum—adding that he hadn't even learned of it until nearly a year later.

I didn't know what to say, how to comfort my former enemy. But this time, thankfully, instead of bullets and bombs, I could at least show him kindness. After all, he was reflecting back on a version of myself I hadn't fully seen until now. I understood—we were more alike than different.

Nghia went on, telling how he'd nearly died that night in a mortar attack. "The Americans had made it into our complex one night," he said. "It startled everyone. We fired, but we could not see our targets. There were grenades—many grenades—killing several of us.

I listened for only a few moments before I recognized what he was speaking about.

S/Sgt. Dever, Lt. Doane, and Steve Charbonneau had slipped through the enemy perimeter and into their bunker complex late one night—around 0200 hours. Their mission, submitted by Lt. Doane and approved by S-2, was to confirm what he suspected—that the enemy was vacating their positions at night to avoid artillery and mortar fire, knowing we had their coordinates.

If the complex had been empty, Doane's plan was to bring the rest of Alpha Company forward before first light and occupy those same bunkers—setting an ambush for the enemy when they returned at dawn. But the complex was not empty. They heard movement. Nothing clear at first. Then—whispers in English. That was all it took.

The position was compromised. AK-47s and SKSs erupted, firing blindly into the darkness. The element of surprise was gone.

The team had no choice but to break contact immediately and move out—fast—before the perimeter closed in around them.

As they withdrew, they dropped grenades into bunkers and fighting positions as they passed—leaving chaos behind them.

When they made it back to our perimeter, Lt. Doane wasted no time. He called for the fire mission.

We had been alerted beforehand and were already standing by. As soon as we heard the contact on Hill 1064, we prepared several rounds in total darkness.

Within moments, I was hanging rounds and firing on command.

Nghia continued, "Not long after the Americans broke contact with our perimeter, the mortars began. I heard them launch… then come in… and explode."

The tremors rolled across the mountaintop. One of them struck our ammo storage area."

By now, it felt like a transparency had slid down perfectly over the map in my brain. Before me sat the man I once believed I'd killed—the man I counted among the dead when my unit breached the top of Hill 1064.

I remembered the adrenaline rush of battle, the almost twisted thrill of knowing how much harm we were inflicting on the enemy. What I did not know—what I could not have known—was that some of that harm had belonged to the very man in whose home I now sat.

War wasn't personal. It was business. Soldiers fighting soldiers. Not part of an ideal world, but the world we were forced to live in. And that didn't make the enemy less. It made them more. Not just fighters. Human beings.

Nghia spoke of three from his village who had joined the army together in 1965. He and his friend Le Thang had already fought the French back in 1952–1956. They had worked the fields together. Done construction together. They were patriots, and their families had encouraged them to return to uniform after unification was denied following the French departure.

Le Thang's specialty was ambush tactics, and he trained young North Vietnamese fighters in that art. He and Nghia served in different units, but both fought the Americans from the same hill. One day, Le Thang had to take his men through an open area—at the same time, American planes dropped napalm.

Le Thang became a living torch—his body consumed in seconds. His flesh twisted and melted like beef thrown on a white-hot fire. His face and arms were disfigured. His legs were stripped of skin until they looked like charred bones, trying to hold him up.

He lived—but he lived as something unrecognizable, like a creature out of a horror movie. And still, Nghia did not harbor hate. Even knowing it had been my unit that pushed his friend to that edge of death.

My mind drifted to what our own troops had endured. I remembered a Marine we called "Sugar Bear," a point man who tripped a booby trap and lost both legs before being shipped home. He lived, too. And while he wasn't disfigured like Le Thang, his maimed body carried the same message. War was merciless. Brutal. It chewed men up—on both sides—and left them to figure out what it meant to keep living.

This time, it was me who fought back the tears—because we mirrored each other, I realized we hurt ourselves as much as we hurt one another. And now, to think of all this—me and Nghia meeting, speaking, understanding—it's nearly beyond my grasp, all because of one poem that refused to stay bound to a page, transferring itself into flesh and blood, into a heart that never expected to hold it.

Nghia and Paul holding the diary that brought us together inside Nghia's house.

It was enough talk for both of us. We sat together, simply enjoying each other's company, until Smith and his assistant cameraman, Phil Sturholm, finally turned their cameras off.

There was a three-and-a-half-hour drive back to Hanoi, and I would be visiting with Nghia again the next day. "It's going to be a long day tomorrow," Smith said. "We'd better get going."

Mrs. Nghia handed me a bunch of bananas from their trees, a food I always enjoyed.

On the way back, while eating one, I thought about the odds stacked against former combat enemies becoming friends. I had read about it in other wars—but never from Vietnam. How unfathomable it was… that through so much horror and suffering, a friendship like ours could even exist. The day had been productive. But more than that—it had changed me.

Somewhere along the way, without realizing it, something inside me had shifted. I had come searching for answers… and found something I had not expected. I cared deeply for Nguyen Van Nghia. Where there had once been hate… there was now something else. I loved the man. His family. His country. And the greatest surprise of all was this: our connection had not begun where I once believed. Not when his little book came out of the box in the States. Not with the first round I fired at Hill 1064. Not even when I read its translation. No… it had begun much earlier.

On the day we each answered the call to war in 1965. Two men—Two worlds apart. Drawn into the same fire. And though I will never know the exact moment, I believe those callings rose together—side by side, as if from the same unseen hand. The same hand that carried his little book across war, across time, across oceans, the same hand that brought us face to face. The same hand that showed me—we were never as separate as I once believed.

CHAPTER EIGHTEEN

LOVE

As the van turned onto Le Thach Street in Hanoi, on our way to the Government Guest House, I realized what war was all about. Hanoi could have been Tokyo or Berlin, Rome or Cairo, London or Moscow, Paris, Washington, D.C., or even Richmond, Virginia—the capital of the Confederacy during America's Civil War.

But to see the war through the eyes of the man I once fought on the battlefield made me think differently about everything—not just the war, but life itself. I never fully understood that there is a time to be born, a time to die, a time to kill, a time to heal, a time to love, and a time to hate, a time for war, and a time for peace, like my father, Leo, reminded me of early on in this journey. Until the day I met Nghia.

And now here I was in Hanoi—a city I once despised, even though I'd never been here before, and would have destroyed at the issue of an order. Instead of targets, I saw men and women, infants, toddlers, and growing children. Their faces were different, their mannerisms different. But in their hearts, I could see mirrors of my own life—my loves, my fears, my hopes for the future. They wanted peace, not war.

The next day, it was time to return to Nghia's home. Until then, most of the conversation had been between two soldiers. But

I wanted to know what Vu Thi Gai thought about the war and her husband's involvement.

She began speaking, her voice was steady, but there was something in her presence—something older, almost timeless. I told him, "When we first learned his little book was returning, that my prediction has turned out to be true." Then, she turned and said to me, "I'm glad you have done this, Mr. Reed. And I'm thankful you kept his things and the little book so well preserved."

But the way she spoke was different—less like memory, more like prophecy fulfilled. It was as though she had always been waiting for this moment, waiting for her words to catch up to reality.

Then she changed the subject to the years 1965 through 1972, when the skies over Thai Binh were shaken by bombs. "This area was heavily bombed," she said. "I was very scared—very frightened. When we heard the warning that the American B-52's were headed our way, I took the children to the shelter."

I didn't catch her meaning at first about the warning that the Americans were coming. Then she clarified what she meant, "Each time B-52s roared off from Guam and headed toward Vietnam, we heard they were coming from the loudspeakers that shook the city."

That's when I spoke up, "It must have been the hardest part, not to mention your husband being gone."

Her answer split the room wide open. "No. That wasn't the hardest part."

"It was the death of my husband," she said, wiping her tears with trembling hands.

A jolt ripped through me and everyone present. Her voice trembled. The air thickened like fog. The film crew froze, cameras poised but motionless, like even they weren't sure if they had the right to keep rolling.

My chest caved. "Wait a minute—did I miss something?" I blurted out, the words tripping over themselves.

I couldn't believe it was the look on my face. Not again. My mind shot back to the fear I'd carried the day before—that maybe this wasn't the man at all, maybe I'd been fooled. Was her husband dead? But he was sitting in the same room. Breathing the same air.

Smith leaned over, steady as a stone, and whispered, "This is the right Nghia."

But Vu broke anyway. She collapsed into sobs—deep, body-shaking sobs that dragged the whole room down with her. Not one of us breathed. We were waiting, every man in that room certain something was about to be torn open.

In her weeping, I could almost see the flashback she was re-living. The day in 1968 when soldiers came into the rice paddy with the news. The letter in their hands. The words that shattered her world. She had dropped to her knees in the mud, neighbors rushing to her, carrying the same kind of letter, the same kind of grief.

It wasn't so different from the stories I'd heard back home—of the American wives standing frozen in their doorways when a car pulled up, two men in uniform stepping out, a telegram in hand. The wives of pilots. Helicopter crews. Infantrymen. Their knees would give out before the words even left the officer's mouth.

That was the grief spilling out of Vu now. The grief of every soldier's wife, no matter which side of the ocean she lived on. Finally, she found the strength. Nghi's voice carried the weight as he translated.

"Two years later… Nghia walked back through their front gate. That is when she learned he had not died."

My mouth went dry. "What? You thought your husband was dead for two years—but he wasn't?"

Her eyes burned through her tears, bringing tears to mine. "Yes… for two whole years… I carried that grief. I almost… wasted away from it. Everyone around me told me to move on—my mother, my friends, the other women in the village. But I would not. Something inside me, refused to believe it. I held on."

After a brief pause, her voice dropped to a whisper. "When he finally came hobbling toward our patio, I thought it was his ghost. I wouldn't go near him. But he kept coming closer, and closer, until I saw it—it was really him. Alive. As alive as any man could be."

Her tears suddenly broke into a smile, and mine too. "We ran to each other. And we held on, and held on."

I finally understood that love was not softness or romance. It was not even affection. Love was endurance. Love was recognition. Love was the refusal to let go of what still had life in it.

Loving—to love—is the ability to see potential in another human being, in yourself, even in broken things, and to care enough to help that life become what it was meant to be. Vu had loved Nghia through death. Nghia had loved his family through jungle and blood.

And somehow, that same force had crossed oceans, wars, and decades—until it reached into my hands.

The whole room sat in stunned silence. Until, of course, Smith leaned over, a smirk tugging at his lips, and muttered, "Told you so."

Apparently, the confusion about his death came around the time Nghia's unit was in combat with mine. The night before my unit captured his diversionary camp and rucksacks, Nghia had been dragged to an underground field hospital, and everyone who stayed on Hill 1064 died the next day.

Since everyone in his unit reportedly died, it was assumed he had too. Nghia's military unit in Thai Binh was notified that his unit had been eliminated, and a request was made to report his death to the next of kin, his wife.

She faced many emotional difficulties; she told the group. The first was the loss of her husband—a tragedy beyond measure for a couple deeply in love. Secondly, there was the shock related to the people's culture. The stigma against being over thirty and female in Vietnam. A widow who is thirty or younger is considered desirable and will often remarry. As a widow over thirty, she was shunned by men seeking wives.

She faced many emotional difficulties; she told the group.

"At night, I would have dreams—nightmares—that he actually died," said Vu Thi Gai. "My life at home was such a struggle, so lonely, and the bombing only made things worse.

Nghia continued, "Sometimes I would dream about battles. It was very terrible and very fierce. Why did the Americans come? And why did I have to live like that in the jungle? It was a very hard life. "At night, I felt very sad," said Nghia, speaking of the same time when he was frequently too far from home to be able to help his family.

"So far away from home. So empty.

Vu Thi Gai interrupted, "Before going south, he was a very strong and handsome man. But after returning home, he was a very weak and wounded man, and yet, I was very, very happy to see him again and to know that we had survived the war. I thought from then on, my family would be unified. Now husband, wife, and children could join together. It's a very warm and good feeling."

Nghia had other thoughts, though. He had nothing to show upon his arrival home, proving his love for her during the years they spent apart.

The poetry he had written about his love for her had been lost forever—until the day the little diary made its way back.

CHAPTER NINETEEN

BLOOD OF MY BROTHERS

Nguyen Van Nghia and I were scheduled to return to the battlefield where we had first, unknowingly, encountered each other. It would be the first time either of us had set foot there since the war. For Nghia, it would be his first plane ride.

Before we left, he wanted to show me how completely he accepted me. He took my hand in his and walked me through his village, smiling at friends, holding me up proudly. Nghia was making a statement—that this American was honored, that this American was his brother. The gesture made me uncomfortable, but later Nghi explained that, in Vietnamese culture, it was the deepest sign of friendship and respect.

Getting to Kontum wasn't simple—the province was off-limits to visitors because of the thousands of unexploded ordnances (UXOs) still in the ground. But when the governor heard our story—two former enemies who had chosen forgiveness, reconciliation, and friendship—he made a rare exception. He granted us permission to climb Hill 1064.

On our way to the battlefield in Kontum

When our plane touched down at Pleiku—boots hitting the tarmac—Nghia turned and said something that froze me in place. "The first time I came here, it took me four months walking the Truong Son range. Today, only an hour and a half."

Incredible perspective, but on this day, we arrived together at Kontum.

The Kontum People's Committee chairman, moved by our story, provided a nine-seat van for the film crew and us, and provided us an excort who was all too familiar with the lay of the land—a former PAVN soldier, a Major.

Turns out, he had been in the AO for some battles with the 173rd Airborne during my and Nghia's timeline.

As we rode toward Hill 1064, the tension was thick with memory. I could see it in Nghia's eyes and feel it in my own chest.

When the van stopped, the hill rose before us. Memories came flooding back. The ridge where Nghia's bunker once stood was faintly visible, but everything else had changed. The tall hardwood trees were gone. The jungle canopy thinned. The battlefield stripped of its teeth.

The last time I'd been here, every second of every day, the enemy threatened my life. Panic seized me at first—thoughts flooded my mind about no weapon, my exposure, and how to defend myself if something broke out. But then I forced my focus back to the present—peace, not war. Still, instinct is instinct. At the bare minimum, it reminded me that what happened here twenty-five years earlier would not be easily forgotten.

As we climbed, my body betrayed me. I caught myself glancing at the ground, half-reaching for tripwires, remembering that ambushes happen when least expected. Then it hit me—Nghia was probably feeling the same. With an outstretched hand, I invited him to pause beneath a bamboo thicket.

Two men—once lethal warriors—once mortal enemies—who had fought with every intention of killing the other, now sat side by side beneath a bamboo thicket. A thicket that could just as easily have been the same one we crawled through in the war. But this time there were no rifles, no bullets. Only two men, scarred by the past, bound now by something far stronger than hate—friendship. The kind of moment I once would have thought impossible—unthinkable—yet here it was—undeniable.

By the look on his face, Nghia was rattled. His eyes darted right, then left.

I asked quietly, "What was the most frightful thing for you in the jungle?"

"Tigers," he said.

Death had always been grunt's work for us—loading bodies into bags, hauling them onto choppers. But PAVN troops had no choppers, no body bags. Their dead were buried right where they lay, and quickly, in shallow graves.

"Tigers would sniff out the burials," Nghia whispered, "and eat them."

"These were your buddies from the Truong Son trail?" I asked.

"Yes," he answered, eyes far away, swallowed by the jungle again.

Near the summit of Hill 1064, the ground felt sacred. The soil still carried what we left there—the greatest violence either of us had ever known.

With cameras rolling, Nghi coaxed him to speak. "We fought and died here," Nghia said. "At first, when we heard the helicopters, we thought it was the First Cavalry. But when we recovered two American ID cards, we knew it was the 173rd Airborne."

Nghia speaking about his experience fighting at Hill 1064m summit where his bunkers were located. Bunker is behind him and camera crew.

When Nghia finished, I felt the weight of what he said settle in my chest.

The 173rd Airborne Brigade made a name for itself in this war. We were the first U.S. Army combat brigade to step onto Vietnamese soil in May of 1965. Volunteers turned into paratroopers. Men trained to move fast, strike hard, and hold ground that others could not. We learned early that nothing in this country came easily—every ridge, every trail, every patch of jungle was earned in blood.

We fought at Hump. We fought and died at Dak To. We bled and died on Hill 875, and among many others, on Hill 1064. We walked into places maps barely named and held them with our bodies. By the time the war was done, nearly eighteen hundred men, all of them our brothers, were dead, at a cost that rivaled any airborne unit in American history. Thirteen Medals of Honor would be pinned on Sky Soldiers. Several Distinguished Service Crosses, Silver Stars, and thousands of Purple Hearts and Bronze Stars would follow us home.

But what the citations never recorded was the weight:

- The weight of carrying men off hillsides.
- The weight of writing letters that would never be answered.
- The weight of knowing that the ground beneath your boots had already learned how to kill.

We were young. We were proud. We were deadly. And we paid for every inch. So, when Nghia said, *"We knew it was the 173rd,"* I understood what he meant.

His commanders in Hanoi had studied us. His unit had learned our patterns, our fire, our stubbornness. They knew who was coming. And we—walking up that ridge in Kontum in 68'—

had no idea that on the other side stood men just as disciplined, just as committed, just as ready to die.

Two elite formations. Two nations' sons. Both forged for sacrifice.

One small hill between us.

Hill 1064 was about to remember us both.

Nghia continued, "We knew of your battles, especially Dak To in '67. Our experts in Hanoi studied them. The 173rd had a fierce reputation. When contact ended here, everyone in my unit was dead. Soldier by soldier, they fought and fell. All of my friends were killed."

On this day, the land was silent. Peaceful. Banana trees and mountains in every direction, green and lush. Nature had painted over it all. I stepped away from the crew. Smith followed with the camera.

I told him, "I can hear the land saying, '*The blood of your brothers was spilled and cries out.*'" I went on. "I once heard that people either run to the source of their pain or run from it. That choice determines whether we begin healing or remain in denial. I'm not running anymore. My pain doesn't control me. I control it."

Then Nghia walked up and broke his own silence. He lifted his shirt and pointed. "This spot—this is where a mortar opened my insides."

The record backs up what my memory already knew.

UNCLASSIFIED

~~CONFIDENTIAL~~

DEPARTMENT OF THE ARMY
OFFICE OF THE ADJUTANT GENERAL
WASHINGTON, D.C. 20310

IN REPLY REFER TO
AGAM-P (M) (30 Jul 68) FOR OT RD 682301 19 August 1968

SUBJECT: Operational Report - Lessons Learned, Headquarters, 173d Airborne Brigade, Period Ending 30 April 1968 (U)

AD392519

SEE DISTRIBUTION

"This document [illegible] affecting the National Defense of the United [illegible] within the meaning of the Espionage Laws, [illegible] U. S. C., Section 793 and 794. [illegible] transmission or the revelation of its contents in any manner to an unauthorized person is prohibited by law."

1. Subject report is forwarded for review and evaluation in accordance with paragraph 5b, AR 525-15. Evaluations and corrective actions should be reported to ACSFOR OT RD, Operational Reports Branch, within 90 days of receipt of covering letter.

2. Information contained in this report is provided to insure appropriate benefits in the future from lessons learned during current operations and may be adapted for use in developing training material.

BY ORDER OF THE SECRETARY OF THE ARMY:

Kenneth G. Wickham
KENNETH G. WICKHAM
Major General, USA
The Adjutant General

1 Incl
as

DISTRIBUTION:
Commanding Generals
US Continental Army Command
US Army Combat Developments Command
Commandants
US Army War College
US Army Command and General Staff College
US Army Adjutant General School
US Army Air Defense School
US Army Armor School
US Army Artillery and Missile School
US Army Aviation School
US Army Chemical School
US Army Civil Affairs School
US Army Engineer School
US Army Infantry School
US Army Intelligence School
US Army Chaplain School

DDC
SEP 20 1968

Regraded unclassified when separated from classified inclosure.

~~CONFIDENTIAL~~

UNCLASSIFIED

Front page of the U.S. Army Operational Report – Lessons Learned, Headquarters, 173rd Airborne Brigade (February–April 1968). This report records the same actions on Hill 1064 that Nghia and Paul would later stand upon together.

> *In the early hours, under mortar harassment,* **A & D Company, 1st Battalion, 503d Infantry** *moved* **north-northeast toward Hill 1064** *with* **D Company in the lead.** *The report says contact was made with* **NVA in bunkers** *at* **vicinity ZB 034010,** *with* **1 U.S. KHA** *and* **2 U.S. WHA** *recorded in that clash. Not long after, it notes D Company taking* **small arms, automatic weapons, and mortar fire** *at* **vicinity ZB 037011,** *costing* **10 U.S. WHA.** *Later, it states* **A & D/1-503 returned to Hill 1064** *and found* **"half a dozen NVA dead,"** *and* **recovered U.S. bodies** *from the earlier fight.*
>
> *(Operational Report / Lessons Learned, February 1968.)*

I cringed—his scars were real—brutal. I remembered our fire mission—crushing their position. We sent so many mortars so quickly that there was almost no chance of survival for anyone unlucky enough to be there.

In a blink, I was back—round after round, the thump of the tube, explosions in the distance, the sky splitting open with fire. I remember thinking, *Keep it coming. Keep pounding that ridge.*

Then it was gone—just like that. Silence smothered the jungle, and the only sound left was the hammering inside my chest.

While Nghia and I never went into great detail about his wounding—or the ordeal of being dragged through agony into pitch-black darkness to their underground hospital—I carried the certainty that he knew it had been at my hand. The silence between us spoke louder than words. I felt guilt-heavy, unshakable. Yet he answered it not with blame, not with bitterness, but with quiet grace. A grace I did not deserve, and one I will never forget.

The fact that he never said a word about his experience made him the kind of man this world rarely sees—more noble than words could ever express. Neither of us needed to say it out loud. That both of us lived was remarkable. That we became friends was truly miraculous.

Then something happened that neither of us had planned. Without a word, we both moved—almost as if led by the same unseen rhythm. In near-perfect harmony, we stood and faced each other. Our eyes locked. The years, the battles, the dead, all pressed in around us. Then, as if acknowledging not just each other but everyone who had never walked off this hill, we raised our hands in salute to one another.

It was not a soldier's salute of orders and commands. It was something deeper. A farewell to war. A recognition of the men we had been—and the men we had somehow become.

As soon as we dropped our salute, we turned our backs to the place of death and walked hand in hand down the hill. That scene of the two of us said everything words couldn't begin to describe.

Sometimes I wonder if Nghia and I had already met—long before Kontum. Not in flesh, not in uniform, but in some unseen way. As if his words were already traveling toward me while I was still a boy in Texas. If the war didn't bring us together, but merely revealed what had been set in motion long before either of us chose a side.

On the ride back to Pleiku, I sat in silence.

I kept thinking about the day I chose Nghia's backpack. How my hand reached where it did. How a small book found its way into a box, into an attic, into my mother's hands, and finally into my heart.

- Maybe none of it was random.
- The hill had given up its dead.
- The war had loosened its grip.
- Two former enemies had walked away as brothers.

- They found peace.

And for the first time, I believed the ground itself could heal—that even in the killing fields—flowers might yet bloom.

CHAPTER TWENTY

HATE DISINTEGRATES

Nghia's fake alligator-skin diary carried several poems about the Hien Luong Bridge, the crossing over the Ben Hai River—better known as the DMZ area. Roughly the seventeenth parallel, it wasn't just a line on a map. It was a blade splitting a nation down the middle, leaving a river bleeding. A scar you could walk across, but never without feeling the cut.

Standing at the bridge, Nghia explained, "At that time, there were two different governments. The South was occupied by foreigners, and in the North, we were taught we should liberate the South. I didn't even know what Americans looked like when I first heard the loudspeakers calling for troops to go south."

Then he told me something that gave me the chills. The first poem in his little book wasn't his own—it belonged to a friend already buried by war. Nghia had copied it onto the very first pages, as if pressing his friend's blood into the journal itself. That was one of the sparks that kept him fighting. That was why it guarded the front of his book.

Listening to him, my respect cut deeper. His words weren't about politics. They were about ghosts, about carrying the dead forward, about survival in a place where survival itself was defiance. I could relate to that.

Tran Khanh Phoi, the vice-chairman of the Quang Tri People's Committee, came out to meet us—another man who had once been my sworn enemy—and walked us across the bridge together. On the east side stood a monument to April 30, 1975, the day the war officially ended. But the bridge still felt raw, as if the wound never fully closed.

I couldn't help but think of the American War Between the States—families carved apart, brothers pointing muskets at one another across lines that probably never should have existed. By day, they slaughtered. By night, some crossed the lines to share bread in the dark. The vice-chairman nodded—it had been the same here, a madness that fed on blood and then sat down to eat.

I said quietly to myself, "This is one more way my former enemies and I were reflections of each other—different uniforms, same blood."

From there, the van carried us toward Route 9, climbing into the Truong Son mountain range and into the heart of the Truong Son National Cemetery. They say more than 14,000 of Nghia's countrymen and women are buried there, but numbers meant nothing compared to the sight. Endless rows of markers stretched like a tide of stone rolling over the hills. Each one a name silenced, a body swallowed, a story cut off mid-sentence. The earth itself felt swollen with the dead, as if it had taken in more than it could bear.

Near the center, a shrine rose above the graves, and overhead a sign declared: *"The Homeland Takes Note of The Fallen."* The words did not comfort. They settled on my chest like another layer of soil. The air carried the sweet smoke of incense, but beneath it lingered something heavier—grief so dense it seemed to cling to your clothes, to your breath, to the inside of your lungs.

Paul Reed standing in the cemetery where over 14,000 of Nghia's countrymen are buried.

I didn't know where to put my eyes.

For eleven days, Nghia and I had walked together—through memories of violence, across land still gouged by war. Here, the ground itself seemed to groan. Every step felt like walking across ribs, over bones that hadn't stopped crying.

By the eleventh day, it was our last. In those days, I wept. I had been shaken. Terrified. And yet inside that gauntlet, something gave way. The man I once swore to kill had become the man I now called—against every instinct and every scar I carried—a brother in arms.

I waited for the right moment to tell him what his poems had done for me. How ink on paper had reached deeper than mortar rounds ever could.

"Without your poetry," I said, my voice unsteady, "I don't think I would've changed. I wouldn't have found the courage to forgive you… or the grace to forgive myself."

Nghia smiled and nodded slowly, as though this truth had been waiting between us all along. He said my coming to meet him meant everything in the world.

"But the best part," he added softly, "was my diary coming back to me—just as my wife predicted many years ago."

He placed his hand on its cover. Not casually. Not possessively, but gently. As though it had a pulse. As though something inside the little book still breathed.

For a moment, I saw it the way he did—not as paper, not as a relic of war—but as a witness. A living thing that had crossed oceans, endured silence, survived hatred, and returned carrying two men inside it.

"It was always meant to find its way home," he said.

Then, with a grin breaking through the weight of the cemetery around us, he added, "The other best part was who my long-lost journal had carried back with it when it returned—you."

Our laughter rose up raw and unguarded, cutting through the graves like a sound that didn't belong there—and maybe that's why it mattered. For a moment, it felt as though the living had reclaimed something the war had tried to keep. And in that moment, I understood something I had never been able to define before.

Love is not weakness, it is not sentiment, and it is not romance alone. Love is the ability to recognize potential—in another man, in yourself, even in something as small as a worn-out diary—and to care enough to help it rise to its fullest purpose.

That little book had seen potential in me before I saw it in myself.

And standing there beside the man I once called enemy, I realized we had done the same for each other.

And hate—quietly, without ceremony—began to disintegrate.

The next afternoon, back in Nghia's village, we exchanged presents. His family, knowing how I had torn through every banana they set in front of me, handed me a bunch to carry. Simple and honest, the kind of gift that stays with you, because it came from the heart.

And then, in the quiet between us, I pinned my silver paratrooper wings on Nghia's chest. It was the most personal gift I had to give—metal that had been my companion as I jumped out of airplanes and into war. A soldier's honor, hammered into shape, now pressed against the shirt of the man who had once been my enemy. In that moment, the wings became a confession: *you are no longer my enemy—you are my friend.*

Later, standing near the van, I looked at Vu Thi Gai and the others and forced my Texas drawl through the words, "Tam biet, hen gap lai, cang som cang tot." Goodbye, see you again, the sooner the better. My tongue bent the words clumsily, but when she repeated them back, smiling, I knew she understood. I was the last to climb into the van.

Reed's says goodbye to Nguyen Van Nghia's wife, Vu Thi Gai

About thirty minutes into the long, jolting drive toward Hanoi, Nghi broke the silence. He had a way of holding things back, choosing when to hand over the truth. This time, he didn't keep it in, "Mr. Reed," Nghi said, pausing, "this is what Vu Thi Gai told me as we were leaving: 'You know, before I thought… because my husband is often sick, and was wounded, he could not remember very well what happened during the war. But when we received word about his lost pack, and the American named Paul Reed brought back her husband's poetry and other items… our family was very, very happy.'"

Her words pinned me harder than the wings I had just fastened to her husband's chest. They sank in and stayed.

Back at Noi Bai Airport, waiting to board a flight to the US, I remembered the report I had obtained through a FOIA request, "Operations Report—Lessons Learned." Declassified and stored away in the records archive in Washington, D.C., it gave the cold particulars of the very battle that had bound Nghia and me together: date, grid, outcome. Paper language for blood. I chuckled to myself—since Vietnam, I'd gone through a few "Lesson-learning operations" of my own.

"Do you think he'll remember me?" I asked Smith.

Smith responded with authority, "I know he will. What you did—that kind of thing doesn't get forgotten."

There was a pause between us before he asked, "I can see the cogs turning, Reed. What are you carrying right now?"

I never gave him an answer. Just looked down at my boots. The diary and the wings came to mind—two emblems that once fed hate and fury, now forging themselves into forgiveness and an uneasy kind of peace.

But there was something else I carried too—heavier still.

I kept seeing Nghia's eyes. The way he squinted. The way he leaned forward, straining to make out the small photographs and documents I had placed in his hands. He would tilt them toward the light, bring them almost to his face, blinking hard as if willing clarity to return.

"What's wrong with your eyes?" I asked him. He didn't hesitate.

"The defoliant Agent Orange. When the airplanes sprayed, it got in my eyes. It burned them."

He said it simply. No accusation. No bitterness. Just a fact. But I felt it.

Airplanes overhead. Chemical mist drifting down. Burning eyes in a jungle already on fire. Agent Orange dropped by our side.

The war had already taken his youth, nearly his leg, and years from his wife and children. and nearly his leg. Now the war was taking his sight—slowly, quietly, over time.

I couldn't sit with that. On the flight home, I couldn't shake the image of him leaning toward the light. The diary in his hands. The man who once stood against me on a hilltop, now straining just to see. And that's when the thought in my head stopped being a thought and became a decision.

What if I could bring him to America? What if I could get him some much-needed medical care? What if a cornea transplant could restore even part of what the war had burned away?

It didn't feel like charity. It didn't feel like generosity. It felt like responsibility. A debt owed. And maybe—just maybe—a small act of love strong enough to push back against what that war had done.

CHAPTER TWENTY-ONE

WELCOME TO AMERICA

Wheels down at Noi Bai. It had been three years since I first landed in Hanoi. In those three years, I had put together a plan—quietly, deliberately—to bring Nghia to America on a healing journey for his eyes. Maybe a cornea transplant. Maybe treatment for chemical damage. I didn't know what would be possible. I only knew I had to try.

And I could still hear Smith on that long flight out, leaning in and asking me, "What are you carrying right now?" Back then, I didn't have an answer. But I did now.

I was carrying more than a passport and a plan. I was carrying the uniforms we once wore. The scars we still bear. Once, those uniforms marked us as men sworn to opposite flags. Once, those scars divided us. Now they bind us. What was meant to separate us had become the very thing that tied us together—in a friendship no flag could have ordered, and no war could have imagined.

As we taxied toward the gate, I turned to Smith and said, "He's taught me more than I ever imagined. More than I'll ever forget." I paused. "His diary opened my eyes. It let me see clearly for the first time since the war. If there's anything I can do to help open his—so he can see clearly again—I'm going to do it."

The highway out of Hanoi toward Nghia's house hadn't changed much. Farmers still rattled past on old tractors, bicycles stacked high with impossible loads—pigs, baskets, bundles of firewood—wobbling but never tipping. They claimed their piece of the road, traffic honking and grinding behind them, drivers leaning on horns in a hurry to get somewhere.

Dust hung in the air, exhaust mixing with the sweet rot of fruit stands and the sharp bite of gasoline. Mom-and-pop stalls still lined the roadside, tin-roofed whatnot shops with hand-painted signs, selling bottled water, canned drinks, cigarettes, trinkets—anything to pull a few coins from the stream of travelers hurrying past.

Thai Binh City, capital of Thai Binh Province, looked much the same, only with more cars on the streets. One big change hit me hard—the old ferry across the Red River was gone. In its place stood a new bridge, concrete and steel, carrying traffic across at highway speed. No more waiting in long lines at the riverbank, no more merchants hawking everything under the sun—dog hindquarters strung up beside cheap trinkets—gone with the ferry.

Tay Giang Village, where Nghia lived, worked, and played, sat just twelve miles out from the city. Easy enough to reach. Finding his house wasn't. After a few wrong turns, the van finally rolled up on a small crowd in the road—Nghia, Vu Thi Gai, family, and a handful of neighbors waved us in. Faces shining, eyes wet, their joy hit me before I even stepped out. After all the years, all the miles, there they were—my welcoming committee, and for a moment the weight of war felt lighter.

Nghia wasn't inside the courtyard this time, a nervous wreck, trembling, and wringing his hands like before. No—this time he stood outside, in the little road beside his house, dressed sharp in a brand-new suit and tie, a huge smile spread across his face.

The trip of a lifetime stood before him. It was safe to say none of his fellow villagers had ever dreamed of doing what this man was about to do. Nghia was going to America. He'd heard of the place but knew little about it. Now he was heading straight into the home of his former enemy.

Just before we loaded the van, I grinned and asked if he was ready to eat American food. Nghia, still smiling ear to ear, said he already had. Silence hung for a beat. We glanced at each other, blank, like a deer's eyes in headlights—none of us knew what the heck he meant. Then it hit. He was talking about the C-rations many of us left behind in foxholes—those little green cans of mystery meat—cold, greasy, and tasting like they'd been sitting in a warehouse since World War II. In fact, the ones I ate most often were dated 1944. We ate them because we had to, not because we wanted to. Most of us would trade half our meal just to avoid the worst ones.

Ham and lima beans—the meal that could start a war all over again. The stuff *we* gagged on. And here Nghia was counting them as American cuisine. We exploded and doubled over with laughter, tears running down our cheeks, and then someone cracked, "*Welcome to America, Nghia—hope you like cold beanies and weenies in a can.*"

Wheels down at Dallas/Fort Worth Airport—October 1996. Nguyen Van Nghia, Luong Thanh Nghi, and I stepped off the plane into a wall of veterans, TV cameras, and supporters waiting for us. After more than fifteen hours in the air, we should've been dead on our feet. But the roar of voices, the flash of cameras, the crush of hands reaching out—lit us up.

American veterans welcome Nguyen Van Nghia to Dallas.

The greeters came to witness a friendship they would never have imagined. The veterans present welcomed a former enemy in peace. My brothers from the war opened their arms to Nghia.

Not all were veterans. A ten-year-old girl, Meredith Boyer, held up a sign written in Vietnamese: "*Welcome to America, Mr. Nghia.*" Meredith was the daughter of a good friend who, a few weeks later, would organize a going-away dinner for Nghia. He told me later that seeing the young girl holding the sign was the warmest his heart had ever felt.

Young Meredith holding the sign welcoming Nghia to America.

The crowd and cameras turned it into the biggest photo-op I had ever experienced and certainly the only one that Nghia had stood in. Shutters snapped, flashes burst, freezing the moment again and again.

Nguyen Van Nghia's Dallas, Texas welcome

Soldiers carried cameras in Vietnam—documenting their travels to and from the battlefield—but nothing like what we experienced in Dallas. I remembered what Smith had warned me about: a project of this nature would garner a lot of attention. That came to mind when a newsman stepped up and shoved a microphone in my face.

"Ah, hello, my name is Jim Douglas, with Channel 8 News. I was wondering if you two could spare a few moments?"

"Sure," I said, "but I'm not too good with cameras."

Douglas smiled, "The cameras didn't bite. My interview will be short, but something my newsroom just has to have."

After getting a nod of approval, Douglas readied himself and spoke into the mic, "I just finished researching the history of American wars in the 20th century," then he paused, appearing to wait for my acknowledgment before going on. Once I gave a nod, Douglas continued.

"The wars I researched were World War I, World War II, the Korean War, and the Vietnam War. As far as I could discover, this is the first—and maybe only—time a North Vietnamese combatant, an enemy of the United States, has traveled to the United States for medical treatment for wounds received during the war."

"It took a lot of time to complete my research. Of all those wars, I was able to find an American who had brought a former German soldier to the U.S., and an American who had met his former enemy in London. He had traveled to England to meet the Japanese soldier who was his prison guard in a POW camp during World War II. That one was made into a movie; I believe the name was *To End All Wars.*"

Other than those two, he had not been able to find a single instance that was similar to this one—former battlefield enemies of the Vietnam War connecting through poetry in a tiny book.

"How do you think your fellow Americans will respond to what you're doing, and how an enemy's handwritten diary actually impacted you?" Douglas challenged.

I quickly responded, pointing to Nghia standing beside me, "Well, I don't know about all those wars or all that stuff you researched—but here's what I do know.

"This man here, I'd be proud to share a foxhole with him any day of the week. He's the kind of guy you could trust with your life. He's got more strength, tenacity, and courage in his little finger than many Americans I personally know.

"This man walked over twelve hundred miles—round trip—through the jungle on the Truong Son mountain range trail—what Americans call the Ho Chi Minh Trail—following orders. He nearly died in an underground hospital, where they roughly stitched up his stomach without anesthesia, and then tried to cut off his leg. If that wasn't bad enough, he has lost most of his eyesight. How could you not respect a man like that?

"As far as how his friendship has impacted me, he kept notes of his thoughts and poetry in that little journal you mentioned. You might say—it opened my eyes. Not just to him. But to the fact that the man I once called an enemy loved his wife, missed his family, and feared death just like I did. It made me see his humanity. And maybe my own."

Douglas then says, "And now, in a certain sense, you are helping to open his eyes."

"I hope so. Because he opened my eyes long before I even thought about helping him with his. He helped me see what most combat vets never get to see—the humanity of the man on the other side. If I restore only some of his sight, it still won't equal what and how his words have restored me.

"Yeah," I said. "That's it. That's it in a nutshell."

Douglas wrapped up the interview, and he and his crew went on their way. Nghia and I were scheduled to see an eye doctor, so we had to leave as well.

After the examination, the doctor determined that the damage to his eyes was not due to chemical poisoning—as was believed—but more similar to wounds received from a concussion; in other words, the damage to his eyes was probably caused by exploding ordinances (EOs).

I asked the Doctor, "You mean the effect of being too close to mortars as they explode?" The doctor nodded his head in agreement.

Luong Thanh Nghi (R) and Dr. Bob Pansick (L) discuss Nghia's eye examination while Nghia (M) seems hopeful the news is good.

A man was watching the evening news from his sofa at home and was intrigued by the interview Douglas had conducted. He decided to contact the TV station the next morning.

"Hello, this is Doctor Van," the voice with a Vietnamese accent said. "I saw an American man on your newscast. He brought a Vietnamese man to the U.S. for medical care. They were enemies, but now they are friends. Can you put me in touch with the American?"

The person at the station received permission and gave him my phone number. The next day, I received a call.

"Reed, is this Paul Reed?" the doctor asked.

I responded, Yes, this is Paul."

"I saw your story on the nightly news. I am originally from South Vietnam, but came to America to attend medical school. I am currently a cardiologist."

I responded, "Yes, we brought him here to try and improve his eyesight, which we think he lost during the war. We are trying to do everything we can to restore his eyesight."

The doctor interrupted, "Well, that's actually along the lines of why I'm calling."

Cutting him off, I said, "There is something I needed to make clear—not out of doubt, but out of honesty. I learned years earlier how sensitive old divisions can be. Doctor," I said carefully, "I want to make sure you understand—Lieutenant Nghia served with the North Vietnamese Army."

There was a brief pause.

"You do understand that, don't you, sir?"

I asked him this—not as a challenge, but simply to be certain we were all standing on the same ground, and there would be no surprises.

"Mr. Reed, though I grew up in the south, in Hue City, I think bringing the man to America was good, and I would like to help.

"How so?" I asked.

"I am willing to give Nghia a full physical and stress test, completely free, of course."

I thought about what he said for a moment, then said, "I'd like to meet you in person, and if I decide to take you up on your offer, we can make concrete arrangements at that time."

Our time with Nghia in America was at a premium, so I had to be careful not to overcommit. I shared the Doctor's offer with Smith, who had allotted a certain amount of time for our filming. He thought it was a great idea and immediately agreed that the check-up or physical should be part of the film.

In the meantime, Nghia and I were scheduled to fly to Washington, D.C., where we visited the Vietnam Veterans Memorial. In quiet solitude, we viewed the wall. I pointed to some of the names I personally knew who had died in the Battle of Hill 1064.

If Nghia was uncomfortable while viewing the names of over 58,000 Americans who died in the war, he managed to keep it a secret. Which I could understand.

However, that did not appear to be the case when we approached the Three Servicemen Statue in bronze by Sculptor Frederick Hart. Nghia froze the instant we came within a few feet; there was no doubt their image spoke to him.

Three Servicemen Statue in bronze by Sculptor Frederick Hart

While he stared, I stepped back and let him have the moment all to himself. I had heard most of my life that one could not judge a book by its cover, but Nghia's face was a cover I believed I could not only judge but also relate to.

I knew for a fact that Nghia had experienced war much more harshly than I had—the reminders of that war were standing directly in front of him, and it showed. This time, it wasn't a wall that held him spellbound. It was the images, the visuals. They elicited some deep, deep emotions.

As we turned to leave, he said, "They are so real, they look exactly like soldiers I saw in the jungle. War is death. War means death."

Next, we visited the White House and then the Vietnamese Embassy, which was not open in 1993 when we first met.

Nghia was thrilled to see not only the White House but where congress meets as well.

Diplomatic relations with North Vietnam did not normalize until 1995, the year the Vietnamese embassy was first opened. Their first ambassador's name was Le Van Bang, and his assistant was

Le Dzung. Both men listened with great excitement as translator Nghi explained how the friendship between two former enemies came about because of a tiny journal. Ambassador Le Van Bang commented that the two of us had shortened his expected duty in America. "Thanks to you, you've made my job easier," he said.

Nguyen Van Nghia's visit to Washington, D.C.

Upon returning to Dallas, we learned that Dr. Van had scheduled Nghia for a physical examination at Medical City of Dallas. After a short ride to the doctor's office, Nghia was introduced to an American tradition—paperwork. Translator Nghi helped answer a bunch of questions since Nghia was not a U.S. citizen.

Smith was there too, securing releases from various assistants who would be part of the film. The two assistants working directly for Dr. Van, who were also Vietnamese and from South Vietnam, agreed to assist the doctor but asked Smith not to use their images in the film. Smith also had to obtain permission to film inside the operating room, which the management of the Medical City of Dallas readily provided.

On the operating table, the nurses prepared Nghia for an angiography. The doctor made an incision in his right upper thigh, planning to insert a small camera mounted on the end of a thin, flexible tube. The camera would provide a view of Nghia's blood vessels and identify any cardiac problems.

However, after many attempts, Dr. Van could not insert the camera. He poked and poked, but couldn't feed the tube into the vessel where the incision had been made. At that point, a frustrated Dr. Van reached for the X-ray machine and snapped an image. Hoping to see how best to navigate the vessel. Click…

The Doctor spent a good deal more time as I waited patiently for the nurses to bring Nghia to the recovery room. Once he arrived, I was helping him sip water through a straw when the doctor showed up and said he had some unexpected news.

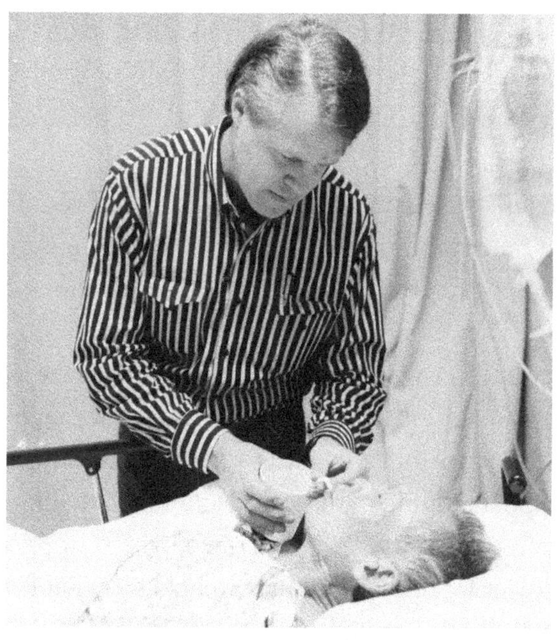

Paul is letting Nghia sip water through a straw at the hospital after Dr. Van performed an angiocardiogram during his full physical examination.

"What is it?" I wanted to know.

"Nghia has a leaking aortic heart valve."

I understood a leaking tire since I was a trucker, but an aortic valve, so I asked the doctor to explain.

"Nghia will never die because of high blood pressure, but while I was attempting to correct the heart valve problem, I encountered a strange situation. I was having a hard time getting the camera to go into Nghia's blood vessel, so I took an X-ray. If I hadn't taken the X-ray and seen it with my own eyes, we would have most likely never seen it. But now it is a matter of fact."

"It what?" I interrupted him anxiously, wanting to learn more.

"When I looked at the X-ray," declared Dr. Van, "I could see why I hadn't been able to insert the tube. Nghia's blood vessel had been cauterized at about the same location where I made the original incision. It was blocked, so I had to make a new incision in the direction of his heart, and once I'd done that, everything worked like clockwork."

By now, I was eating out of his hand. "What are you saying? What does that mean?"

"The main artery coming from Nghia's heart running down his leg had been cauterized. In other words," Dr. Van continued, "he was probably bleeding to death, and the doctors needed to stop the blood flow to his leg. They did that by cauterizing that artery. Once the blood flow to his leg had been severed, he was going to lose the leg except—."

"Now, wait a minute," I said while remembering Nghia's story about how he got wounded in battle—about a mortar round exploding and shrapnel lodging in his right leg. "You're telling me that the main artery in one of his legs got severed, which stopped the blood flow to his lower leg. That would mean he'd lose that leg, right?"

"No, not at all. I mean, I see the X-ray where his artery got cauterized." He said, "That alone would stop the blood flow."

I interrupted, "But he'd get gangrene and die when the poison spread to the rest of his body, yes, no?"

"Not necessarily so," the doctor cheerfully said.

"Wait a minute," I said, motioning for us to step out of earshot from Nghia. I pointed back inside the room where Nghia lay. "If what you are saying is true, he grew a new artery?"

"Yes, it was entirely possible given the set of circumstances during combat, high blood pressure, high excitement, and all. Had his body not been able to do that, he would have died in the jungle," the doctor surmised.

My mind was racing in circles, and I asked again. "You mean the blood flow to his lower leg was totally lost the moment doctors cauterized the artery to stop him from bleeding to death, then mysteriously, a new artery grew back? Is that what you are saying?"

Dr. Van said it plainly, "There's nothing mysterious about it. Under extreme stress, the human body can grow new arteries. High blood pressure. Combat trauma. It happens."

He said it like it was normal science. Like anatomy. Like survival, doing what survival does. But I stood there staring at that X-ray, trying to wrap my mind around what he had just told me.

That artery had been burned shut in the jungle to stop him from bleeding to death. With the blood flow cut off, his leg should have been finished. Any textbook would have predicted that gangrene or some kind of infection would set in, most likely leading to death. Except that's not what happened.

Somewhere in that underground hospital, while mortar rounds were still echoing across Hill 1064, his body made another decision. It built a new road. A new artery. A new way for blood to reach his leg. Had that not happened, he would have lost his leg.

- Had he lost the leg, he never would have walked six hundred miles back through the Truong Son mountains.
- Had he not walked home, he would not have been reunited with his wife and lived to raise his children.

- Had he not lived, most likely my mother would not have opened a dusty box in our attic and felt something in her spirit to tell me to translate a tiny, fake alligator-skin diary.
- I would never have met the man whose words opened my own eyes.

The doctor called it physiology. I called it providence. Because that wasn't just blood finding a way. That was history finding a way. That was a diary surviving long enough to come home. That was two former enemies being kept alive long enough to discover they were brothers. Now that's what I call wealth. Real and lasting wealth.

And whether medicine explains it or not, when the Doctor showed me that X-ray, I knew what I saw. It looked like a miracle to me.

During his stay, we were able to visit one of the largest Vietnamese communities in America, in Los Angeles. Nghia commented, "It looks like we're in Vietnam."

One afternoon, I welcomed Nghia to my office, a place where I spent much of my time at the computer. On the wall, among military awards and medals, hung an NLF or Viet Cong flag, replicas of those removed from his backpack during the war. The flag, too obvious to overlook, was not Nghia's focus. Instead, the American military medals I'd received while on active duty garnered his attention.

"What do they all mean?" he asked while pointing to the medals.

"Well, that one there is a *Bronze Star*, which was for successful ground operations against enemy forces. Guess the enemy would have been you," I jokingly said. "The rifle on the blue background and a wreath, that's a *Combat Infantryman Badge*. A soldier had to be in the infantry to earn one of those."

I intentionally skipped over the Purple Heart and pointed to my *Air Medal*. We got one of those for each twenty-five helicopter combat assaults."

It was clear Nghia didn't understand, but when he saw me pointing to a photo of helicopters in flight, he quickly began shaking his head, saying he understood. In the background of the photo were the hills and valleys so characteristic of Kontum. He pointed and nodded his head up and down.

One by one, he learned the meaning of all the medals. I saved the *Purple Heart* until last. "The army awarded us one of those each time we got wounded." Partially removing my shirt, I showed him the scar on my neck and left shoulder. I told him the scar was from being hit by shrapnel in Binh Dinh Province during a firefight.

When we had first met back in Vietnam as former enemies turned friends, Nghia had mentioned he'd been wounded and dragged to an underground hospital—but he never went into detail. Now, standing in my home in America, beneath the medals of my own war, he lifted his shirt.

He didn't need to point. A scar ran across his abdomen, the full width of his body—the scar was an inch wide, pale and thick, like a seam where death had once tried to open him. I thought he was inviting me into the conversation, but I was wrong. He said quietly that he would prefer to let the past remain in the past, if that was all right.

I offered him a cup of hot tea, which he accepted. We sat staring into our cups. Hot tea has a way of loosening one's memory, and after a long silence, with a tone that carried more weariness than drama, he began to speak.

"It was rough. Very rough," he said. "We had extreme heat during the day and cold in the mountains at night. There were snakes, tigers, disease, and dysentery. Many of our soldiers didn't have shoes, so they issued us sandals made from old tires, but they hurt our feet. Oftentimes, we threw them away and walked barefoot."

I said with a smile, "Ho Chi Minh sandals, that's what we called them."

He continued, "Most of the time, we had no medicine. Many men got malaria. Some became very sick. Disease was one of the leading causes of death. The dead were buried by the side of the trail."

He didn't dramatize it. He didn't have to.

"Several of the men deserted, and when they ventured from camp, it happened—we heard them screaming—they were being eaten alive."

He did not elaborate. He didn't need to.

"If you survived sickness," he went on, "you still had to survive the B-52s. We never knew they were coming until after they hit. It was demoralizing."

I knew the sound they made—I felt them from the other side.

"We timed our meals around American flight patterns. We camouflaged carefully when we rested. More than two million North Vietnamese hiked that trail. Tanks and heavy artillery passed over it. It was five hundred miles. Most plants could not be eaten. Water was often unclean. But it was easier to deal with parasites than to die of thirst."

He spoke not like a victim, but as a man discussing the weather.

"A soldier starting down the trail, well-fed and equipped, could take three and a half to four months to complete the journey. Some days I traveled several miles. Other days, only a few hundred yards."

Then I asked the question that had been eating away in me. "But during contact with the Americans…"

He nodded.

"During that battle," he said, meaning Hill 1064, "I was severely wounded. That was the afternoon your unit captured our diversionary camp and took our backpacks. In the mortar attack, I took shrapnel in my stomach and a gash through an artery in my right leg. That was my last night in combat because I was dragged into an underground hospital nearby."

He paused and let out a sigh, "With stomach and leg wounds, and partial blindness, no one was there to help me. They wanted to amputate my leg, but I pleaded with them. They heated a hot iron rod until it was red-hot and cauterized my leg wound. I thought I was going to die just from the pain.

When I had regained some of my strength, they set me loose in the jungle with only the clothes on my back. I used what I knew as a farmer, and what I had learned in war, to survive."

I felt the room narrow as he spoke.

"I got malaria again, in fact, several times. I would stop. I lived through the chills, the fever. If I didn't reach food or water, I could die. There were many times I did not know if I would recover or die. Once I found food and water, I was able to continue.

Then he said something that did not sound like a former soldier, and he grew quiet before he said it. He was not dramatic. Not theatrical. Just honest.

"One time, I almost gave up."

He described it without embellishment. Fever from malaria. His leg throbbing. His vision blurred from infection and chemical burns. Weak from hunger. Alone, with no unit. No medic. No stretcher. No guarantee of reaching home.

"I was just lying there thinking this may be the place I would stay. The jungle was thick, and the air was wet and heavy. The insects were constantly attacking me. I had no strength left to push to the next ridge. I was ready to stop and let the jungle take me.

"Then something happened and I continued on. I remembered the slogans—*fight to the last bullet, the last drop of blood. Fight for unification and independence.* Many days, those words felt very far away.

"Then one day I stumbled into a dark, bombed-out village with caved-in roofs. The smoke had long cleared, and there was a heavy silence. PAVN soldiers lay scattered where they had fallen. A battle had happened there, but with whom, I didn't know, and it no longer mattered—I was exhausted, I had a fever, I was half blind, and I was all alone.

"Among the dead, I found a pistol still strapped to a corpse. I took it and walked to the edge of a burn pit—the earth was blackened and hollow. I raised the gun to my head and pulled the trigger. I heard the hammer fall. Nothing. The chamber was empty.

"I searched the ground and found a single round. Loaded it with trembling fingers. Brought the pistol back up. My finger tightened. And in that suspended second—between despair and finality—I heard something. Not artillery. Not helicopters. Not jungle noise.

"Her flute. The same melody she had played before I left for the South. Soft and clear. Impossible, I thought, then I froze. The jungle seemed to hold its breath. I lowered the pistol, and it slipped from my hand and hit the dirt. I wiped the tears from my eyes.

"I could see her," he said quietly. "Playing. Waiting for me.

"In that moment, all the slogans meant nothing, but love did and I chose to keep walking."

The image he had painted landed in the room heavier than artillery and surrounded us.

There was no hatred, no politics, no orders, just an incredible memory of her music. His wife, playing the flute, was what carried him and gave him the determination to endure and choose life.

By now, I was actually feeling his pain. Especially when he told me that when he finally reached home, thin, fevered, scarred for life, he stepped through the gate of his village, and Vu looked at him as if she were seeing a ghost.

"The army told me you were dead," she had said.

"For two years, she had carried that grief. For two years, she had mourned a husband who, somewhere in the jungle, in the south, had died. I stood there quietly for a long time before answering her. I was almost dead. Only your flute kept me alive."

"She didn't understand at first, so I explained.

"How I had found the pistol. How I had pulled the trigger. How I had heard the melody she used to play in the evenings before he left for the South.

"I believed you were playing for me," he said. "So, I kept walking."

Vu wept when he told her that. Not because she believed she had physically been there—but because she understood something deeper. Love had reached him where medicine could not.

And whether it was memory, imagination, or something sent from heaven, it had been enough to silence the pistol, bend the course of his life, and keep two former enemies alive long enough to discover they were brothers.

That same day, Dr. Rick Miller, a local dentist friend of mine and a Vietnam veteran, called and expressed interest in donating his time and effort to clean Nghia's teeth and address other dental needs.

Only a day or two later, Nghia was in the doctor's hot seat, his dental chair. Although it was his first time, remarkably, he had no cavities.

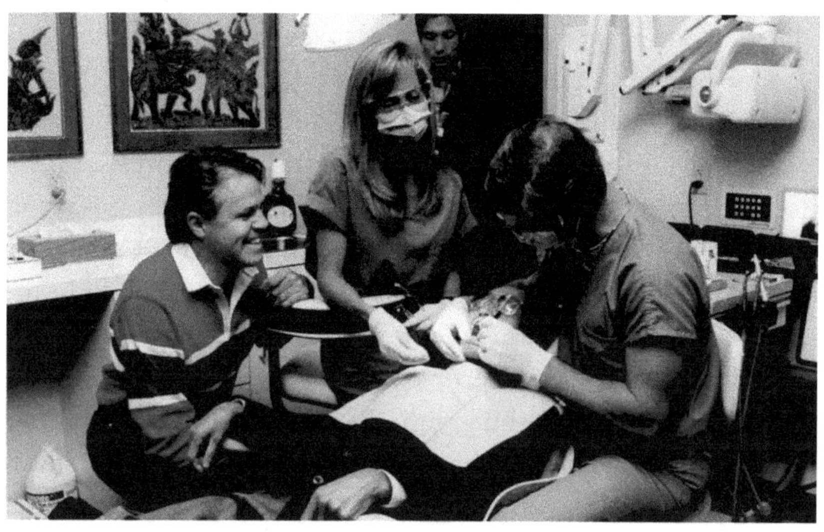

Nghia's first-ever visit to the dentist for a cleaning. Left to right: Paul, Holly Moshier, Nghia, and Dr. Miller.

When Rick asked what had happened to his two missing canine teeth, everyone had a big laugh. It probably wasn't funny at the time, but Nghia was laughing when he told the story, so everyone laughed with him. When I thanked the doctor for his efforts, he said he was both honored and delighted to have been called upon.

Rick told me later that he was indeed blessed to provide dental care to Nghia, that helping him went beyond anything he'd ever experienced, and that helping this man was a life-changing event he'd carry with him for the rest of his life.

That evening, I got a special call from Fort Worth city councilman Jim Lane. He explained he'd seen the two of us on TV and really enjoyed seeing a former soldier helping his former enemy, especially in trying to improve his vision. He continued, he was a Vietnam veteran himself and was interested in doing something that the man from Vietnam would likely never forget.

"Yes, sir," I said. "What might that be?"

"Well, if you will bring him over to Fort Worth this coming Thursday, we will entertain him and make him feel like he was a genuine born-and-raised-in-Texas individual."

"You're on," I said.

That Thursday, Jim met us on the North Side of Fort Worth, on Exchange Street, near the rodeo arena in the old cattle yards. With him were two Native Americans, Ben Tahmahkera, a Comanche, and Eddie Sanduval, an Apache. A Fort Worth Marshall from the city had also come as part of the welcome crew. They treated Nghia to the steak dinner of his life, or at least one he would never forget.

As dinner was finishing, Jim Lane stood and told Nghia they had a few gifts to commemorate his visit to Fort Worth. First was a ribbon attached to a large key, and as Nghi translated, one could see Nghia's face light up as soon as Jim leaned over and placed an honorary *Key to the City* around his neck.

He understood the optics alright, but Nghi had difficulties translating and pronouncing Jim's words in the drawl known as Texan. As Nghia was handed the citation, making him an honorary citizen of the city, a boy from M.L. Leddy's across the street stepped over and placed a beautiful silver Stetson hat on his head. Right then and there, it was clear Nghia was on the ride of his life—he was an official cowboy.

Just then, he began pointing, seemingly across the street toward the rodeo coliseum where a huge Longhorn steer monument was located.

"What do you want? What do you want?" Nghi asked.

"I want to ride."

"He wants to ride," Nghi said. Jim laughed and laughed, then all of us headed to the coliseum, where Jim personally helped Nghia get on.

If smiles were outward expressions of inward feelings or signs of approval, they were all over Nghia's face as he sat atop that Longhorn. None of us present had ever seen a bigger smile.

On this day, this former soldier who'd fought against the Americans during the war got to see different people. I remembered Nghi, the translator, saying once the war was over, the Americans were no longer Nghia's enemy.

This time, the Americans made him feel appreciated and welcome. And he'd gotten to see a part of Texas he would not soon forget. I concurred with Jim that it was doubtful Nghia would ever forget the kindness they had extended to him on this day.

Before he left to return to Vietnam, I hosted a farewell dinner at a local Vietnamese restaurant in Dallas. Lindi Boyer, Meredith's mother, the little girl who met us at the airport, helped organize the event.

Approximately twenty-five guests showed up to bid Nghia goodbye. The evening was warm, peaceful, and emotional, filled with laughter that carried through the room. Nghia sat in the middle of it all, wide-eyed, surprised by the joy aimed squarely at him.

Later, he told me that his trip to the US was really great, and his treatment unexpected and gleeful, but the sign Meredith had held up for him at the airport was still one of the most heartwarming memories from his entire trip.

The next day, the two of us boarded the plane for Vietnam. I wanted to travel with him back to his home. In Kontum City, twelve miles from Nghia's village of Tien Hai, we were greeted by family members happy to have their journeyer husband, father, and uncle figure home.

Nghia receiving the honorary Key to the City of Fort Worth and a genuine Stetson hat presented by J boy of M.L. Leddy western store in Fort Worth, Texas. Left to right: Luong Thanh Nghi (translator), Nguyen Van Nghia, J boy & Jim Lane.

Nghia's family homecoming greeting in Thai Binh City. L to R: Standing behind Standing behind Nguyen Van Nghia is Luong Thanh Nghi (translator), Nguyen Van Nghia (Nguyen Van Nghia's daughter), and Vu Thi Gai.

Bringing a smile to my face, Vu Thi Gai let it be known she was not sure her husband would ever come back to Vietnam after going to America. The possibility he'd get snatched up by a beautiful woman weighed heavily on her, she said, but she was extremely pleased he'd decided to return home, and it showed.

At a local hotel, we said our goodbyes once again, but the sentiment on our faces told a different story. Goodbye didn't really mean goodbye.

After returning to Dallas, I sat by myself on a park bench beside a beautiful lake. For a long time, I just watched the water and let the noise inside me die down. War had tried to take everything from us—our friends, our years, and our peace of mind. It carved scars into our bodies and left memories that we didn't know how to stop. But sitting there, with Nghia back home safe, I knew something I couldn't have known back in 1968.

War could not destroy everything:

- War could not destroy the part of a man that still knows love.
- War could not destroy the part of a man that can lay down hate.
- War could not destroy the strange, hard-won bridge that now stood between two soldiers who once would've killed each other without a second thought.

I realized I was extremely blessed and thankful that God didn't let either of us die with the kind of hatred I'd once had in my heart for the man, the poet. I just hadn't known the real Nghia.

Then there was my mother's curiosity, the night she brought the box down from the attic—the first time she laid eyes on the tiny book. She turned it over in her hands, wondering what secrets it held.

"You should get it translated," she said.

I had responded that I didn't understand Vietnamese.

"There might be something in there that could change your life for the better. Then you could write a book about it."

The little book had already begun its work. It had called us—Nghia and me—into the war. With perfect timing, it guided each of us to the exact ground where we would clash—as enemies without either of us knowing a guiding hand was at work. The little book brought us to Hill 1064—cursed, blood-soaked, littered with our dead—and with it great grief. It locked us in silence and pain for two and a half decades—scars that never healed, nightmares that never quit, grief that never let go. And then the little book carried us back, face to face, not in combat but in peace. Not just to remember. Not only to be remade, but to fix the wrongs between us, and to begin healing our two nations.

And then—suddenly I heard Nghia's voice...

LOVE

Love bears no grudge.
It is not a butterfly and flower,
Love endures until old age.
Do not trifle with love, or there will be sorrow.
Do not rush love in order to enjoy it.
Handle love with care;
Be compromising.
Close your eyes, forget about everything.
Calm yourself, listen to the world speak.
Love bears no grudge.

The very poem that had shattered my hatred—and gave me back my soul.

CHAPTER TWENTY-TWO

THE REST OF THE STORY

In 2016, a former American president, President Obama, stood in Hanoi before a hall filled with young Vietnamese and said something that traveled farther than he probably knew—"Let's also not forget that the reconciliation between our countries was led by our veterans who once faced each other in battle."

I wasn't there. But the words found me. Reconciliation led by veterans. Not by diplomats. Not through policy. Men who once tried to kill each other.

Years before that speech, I had returned to Vietnam many times. Not as a soldier. Not even as a guest. As a man retracing the ground where something had lodged itself deep within his soul, and yet offered no answers.

Nghia and I stood once more at the base of Hill 1064. Decades earlier, we had tried to erase each other from the earth on the hilltop we both remembered as death. Mortars. Napalm. Smoke so thick you could taste it.

Now there were no rifles. No steel pots. No radio chatter. No C-rations. Just two men, soon to be out of breath after a long, steep, but quiet climb. We didn't speak much as we moved upward. There are some places where words don't belong.

At the top, the jungle had returned. Most, if not all, of the hardwood trees that towered high above his location at the time were gone. Only bamboo and wind now. No bunkers. No burned earth. No shouting. Just green.

I looked at him. The same man I once imagined killing. The same man who once heard mortars fall on him. We stood there together, not as former enemies, not as symbols, not as representatives of nations. Two former soldiers who had survived long enough to choose something different.

And then he reached out. Not dramatic. Not staged. Just offered his hand and I took it. That was the moment the war ended for me. Not in 1975. Not when the planes lifted off. Not when the guns went silent. It finally ended when the man I once hated stood on the very ground where we had tried to destroy each other—and took my hand.

Forgiveness isn't found in a speech. It isn't forgetting the past. It's the courage to stop carrying a weapon long after the battle is over.

What carried us to that hill was a small, fake alligator-skin-covered diary—once ripped from a backpack in the jungle, once locked in an attic, once translated at my mother's insistence. But what carried us down that hill was something else. It was our choice.

If you are reading this, maybe you are carrying a battlefield of your own. Maybe your enemy has a different face. A different name. A different story. I don't know what you've lost. But I know this—the war only continues if you keep fighting it.

Sometimes the bravest thing a man can do is open his hand.

The hill was green again when we climbed down. And for the first time in a long time—

So was I.

IN CLOSING

The words in this book traveled farther than their author could have imagined—from the steaming jungles of Vietnam, across oceans, through decades of silence, and back into the hands of the man who wrote them. By then, Nguyen Van Nghia and I were no longer enemies. We were two men who had survived the same war from opposite sides.

In these pages, I still hear his younger voice—fierce in duty, tender in love—reaching across time and battle lines. Preserving his poetry here is more than remembrance. It is a bridge that was rebuilt, a promise that was kept.

War took much from both of us. It scarred our bodies. It shaped our nights. It followed us home. But it did not take everything.

It could not destroy the part of a man that still knows how to love. It could not destroy the part of a man that can lay down hate. And it could not destroy the possibility that two former enemies might one day stand as friends. Nevertheless, if you didn't already know, at least now you know the intended reveal of this book—What War Could Not Destroy—it was....

Our Humanity.

If these pages offer anything, I hope it is this—that in the voice of a former enemy, we may hear something of ourselves—and in doing so, discover that even after the worst of war, peace is still possible.

ABOUT THE AUTHOR

From the jungles of Vietnam to the highways of America, Paul Reed's life has been a road marked by survival, transformation, and an extraordinary handshake with a man he had once tried to kill—the North Vietnamese soldier whose captured diary would become the key to forgiveness, healing, and a friendship that defied the past.

That story first began to take shape when Reed was invited by his friend Gary Gullickson, a fellow Vietnam veteran and U.S. Marine, to contribute a short story for his book, *Vietnam: Our Story, One on One*. It was Reed's first taste of writing, and it opened a door he didn't know was there, eventually leading him to co-author *Kontum Diary: Captured Writings Bring Peace to a Vietnam Veteran* with Ted Schwarz.

The book went on to appear on the Military Best Seller list for several weeks following its release in 1996. Its message of forgiveness and reconciliation resonated widely, drawing national attention through television appearances and newspaper coverage—particularly during Nguyen Van Nghia's visit to the United States for medical care, when the two men appeared together and shared their story at book signings in Dallas, Texas.

While co-authoring the book, Reed became an associate producer for two PBS documentaries that told his and his former enemy's story of forgiveness and friendship—not only on television, but also at film festivals in Dallas, Washington, D.C., the United Nations in New York City, and—on behalf of Search for

Common Ground, an international non-governmental organization founded by John Marks, with offices in Washington, D.C., Brussels, Belgium, and Jerusalem—where he introduced his PBS television documentary on forgiveness between former enemies to an audience of more than six hundred Jews, Arabs, and Christians.

The first documentary, *Kontum Diary*, won an Emmy Award, among several other honors. It was followed by a sequel, *Kontum Diary: The Journey Home*, which went on to reach audiences worldwide when NHK Television in Japan acquired exclusive broadcast rights for its national network. Both films have been screened to international audiences—from diplomatic halls to cultural festivals—and many other venues. The two men's reconciliation journey has been chronicled in major U.S. newspapers and countless journals too numerous to mention, as well as in *People* magazine's "Men at Peace," on *Good Morning Texas*, *The Today Show* with Bryant Gumbel, and CBS's *48 Hours* in a program hosted by Peter Van Sant and Dan Rather, titled *The Fight to Forgive*.

Reed has never viewed these accomplishments as personal achievements alone. The real measure of his work lies in the millions of people—across America and around the world—who have witnessed his story of forgiveness and reconciliation.

They, not he, are the true recipients of the message—beneficiaries of a living example that enemies can become friends, and that peace can rise from the ashes of war. Numerous viewers have contacted him to say how the films touched their hearts, helping them find forgiveness, healing, and closure in their own lives.

Reed's newest book, *What War Could Not Destroy*, continues the remarkable story first told in *Kontum Diary: Captured Writings Bring Peace to a Vietnam Veteran*. But unlike the earlier book, *What War Could Not Destroy* reveals the complete, remarkable, and extraordinary story of Nguyen Van Nghia—Reed's former enemy whose tiny, handwritten diary became the bridge that joined two men once divided by war. In its pages, Nghia's and Reed's stories unfold side by side—in almost play-by-play action—two lives once divided by war, now joined in forgiveness and peace.

Reed's military service with the U.S. Army's 173rd Airborne Brigade earned him the Bronze Star, Purple Heart, Air Medal, Good Conduct Medal, Combat Infantryman's Badge, as well as the Vietnam Service and Campaign Medals, and a Jumpmaster qualification. After his honorable discharge, his path led through college, selling Harley-Davidsons, owning and operating a Purina feed store in Fort Worth, and driving interstate trucks hauling produce throughout the Pacific Northwest and Canada.

Over the years, Reed returned many times to Thai Binh Province in northern Vietnam to visit Nghia and his family, often bringing other veterans with him. What began as a personal journey of healing soon revealed a deeper need—one that extended far beyond his own experience.

Having witnessed firsthand the power of reconciliation, Reed recognized that many combat veterans continued to carry invisible wounds long after the war had ended. Determined to help others find the same measure of peace he had discovered, he founded Valor Veterans, a nonprofit organization dedicated to escorting veterans suffering from post-traumatic stress back to the places of their wartime experiences—often facilitating meetings with former enemies, or their families, in an effort to promote healing and understanding.

Through this work, Reed helped create moments of profound reconciliation. Among them was the return of Colonel James Williams, a U.S. pilot who had been shot down over North Vietnam during the war. Decades later, through Valor Veterans, Williams returned to Hanoi. Although the North Vietnamese pilot involved in the engagement had since passed away, the President of the Vietnam–USA Society, Ambassador Nguyen Tam Chien, arranged for the pilot's wife to meet with him. What followed was not a meeting of enemies, but of shared humanity—one that led to an evening together over a traditional Vietnamese meal, where understanding quietly replaced the distance of war.

Reed's efforts have also been recognized internationally. During that same visit, Ambassador Nguyen Tam Chien presented him with a commemorative gift, honoring his role as founder of Valor Veterans and his commitment to helping both American and North Vietnamese veterans find healing in the aftermath of war.

In moments like these, the past no longer stood between former enemies—it stood behind them.

Ambassador Nguyen Tam Chien presents Paul Reed with a commemorative gift in recognition of his work as founder of Valor Veterans, fostering reconciliation and healing between American and North Vietnamese veterans.

Among his most treasured civilian honors are the Hero of Forgiveness Award from the Worldwide Forgiveness Alliance, the Legion of Honor Award from the Chapel of Four Chaplains, and the Veterans Commendation Award presented by former Vietnam POW and U.S. Congressman Sam Johnson, recognizing his service to the country and his ongoing commitment to peace and reconciliation.

Reed remains deeply active in veterans' and military associations and has served as Newsletter Editor for Chapter 13 of the 173rd Airborne Brigade Association, an officer of Chapter 542 of the Military Order of the Purple Heart, a member of Chapter 1122 of the Vietnam Veterans of America, and the 82nd Airborne Division Association's North Texas Chapter, the Military Order of World Wars (MOWW) as a Patriot member, the Disabled American Veterans (DAV), and the Veterans of Foreign Wars (VFW). Through these associations, Reed faithfully serves his fellow active-duty personnel and veterans alike, offering support, advocacy, and a living example of lifelong service.

But for Reed, the true reward has never been the medals or the headlines—it has been the quiet moments when an old soldier's handshake carries more than words, or when an enemy from long ago stands before him as a friend, proving that even in the aftermath of war, peace is possible.

APPENDIX

What follows is the complete translated text of the small book carried by Second Lieutenant Nguyen Van Nghia, a political officer in the People's Army of Vietnam. Discovered by Paul Reed during the Battle of Kontum in 1971, the small leather-bound book held pages of poetry—some written by Nghia, others by fellow soldiers—blending love, longing, duty, and the daily realities of war. In these verses, readers will hear not the voice of "the enemy," but of a son, a husband, a comrade, and a man who, like soldiers everywhere, carried pieces of home into battle. What follows is presented exactly as translated, with minimal interpretation, so that Nghia's words may stand on their own, bridging the distance of decades and crossing the boundaries that once divided us.

It is always difficult to translate poetry from one language to another. Word images and sounds which flow artistically in one tongue are likely to seem disjointed in another language. In this case, such problems are compounded by the radically different grammatical and syntactic structures of Vietnamese and English. Phong ba bão táp không bằng ngữ pháp Việt Nam says in Vietnamese—"No storm rages like Vietnamese grammar."

Vietnamese is a fusion of Chinese, Thai, and Mon-Khmer languages. Thus, it has words from both tonal (Thai, Chinese) and monotonic (Mon-Khmer) languages. Differences in tone, indicated by diacritical marks above or below the words, can result in two entirely different words being spelled similarly. A careless hand (understandable in combat field conditions) might inadvertently omit one of these marks, resulting in confusion for the reader.

Vietnamese words never change in number, gender, person, or tense. But the same word can have different grammatical functions and, depending on its use, many meanings. A word's meaning is also dependent on word order, which can render the liberties taken by amateur poets confusing. In addition, the system of pronouns, one of the most complicated in the world, is very difficult to render in English. Often, the translators' choice of an English pronoun is little more than a matter of opinion.

Because of these difficulties, the reader should be aware that another translator might legitimately offer quite a different translation, even when looking at the same writing. Our translation tries for a middle ground between the most literal possible translation, which would conceal its poetic nature, and a freer translation, which would produce refined English poetry. Thus, it may not do justice to simple soldiers who sometimes labored to put what was in their hearts into appropriate words.

There is a long tradition of journal writing and poetry in Vietnam, and it was not uncommon for soldiers to carry journals in wartime. Due to the fortunes of war, untold thousands of Vietnamese journals fell into American hands. Our soldiers were instructed to turn them over to the authorities, which, after review, were placed in classified files until well after the war.

Years later, they were transcribed to microfilm before being destroyed. One of those diaries currently resides at the *William Joiner Center for the Study of War and Social Consequences* at the University of Massachusetts, Boston. Another, *Poems from Captured Documents*, by Thanh Nguyen and Bruce Weigl, Amherst: University of Massachusetts Press, 1994, contained translations of poems from various diaries.

Lieutenant Nghia's little book held words that reached beyond war—in the traditional sense. He included poems written by several different soldiers as well as many of his own. Unfortunately, he no longer remembers which is which, or the significance of the names and dates at the front of the book, or the dedication at the end. War tore away much of his memory.

The following pages contain a reproduction of the complete diary—and a translation of each page, even when the significance of what has been written is not clear. Note that the poems often extend for more than one page. Others are composed as though written by some other person—someone he knew, a sweetheart from home, or a Southerner.

MEMORIES

(19)67 (month)
Democratic Republic of Vietnam
Hoang (a man's name)
November 26, 1967
Dang (a man's name)
March 5 to March (?), 1965
nighttime March 29, 1965
July 17, 1965
9:30 April 8, 1965

FOR SEVEN YEARS, I HAVE STOOD GUARD AT THE SEVEN-SPAN BRIDGE

For seven years, I have stood guard at the
seven-span bridge,
So many times, I have paced back and forth.
Life overflows on the Northern shore
And spreads to the high sea.
Oars splash to the beat of the rowing song.
Why does the South so move us?

On the Southern shore of the narrow river
The nights are dark and lifeless.
I feel the crying of the people.
I have met many sweet sisters on the Southern shore.
Their sufferings find me on the other side of the seven-span bridge,
Leaving me ever troubled.
Watching the Star Flag billow,
I miss my mother, her warm smile,
In the kitchen tending a fiery stove
On a starry night.
I recall the painful separation
Of a mother from her young son.
For not even a second have I abandoned my post.
I am here for my parents, braving the wind,
A proud soldier of this bridge, of my people.

LITTLE KOREAN BROTHER

Oh, little Korean brother!
Where is your mother?
Where can she be found?
Is there anybody left to ask about
The invaders and war everywhere,
The corpses strewn about?
Snow silently surrounds the villages;
The homes are in ruins and deserted.
Isn't that your mother,
Her white body swinging,
Hair drooping from her skull,
Dangling from the end of a rope?

Isn't that your father,
Hair drooping from his skull,
His gaunt body covered with blood?
No, not so, my little brother!
Your mother is here,
A laborer transporting ammunition
Here is your mom; she is a nurse.
Your father is here on the battlefield,
Face blackened by gun smoke
Blocking the enemy's retreat.
Your older brother is here.
Your volunteer brother.
I am glad to be beside you, big brother.
Together with Father, we will slay all of the barbarians
So our motherlands can rebuild.
So our sisters can be happy
And sing in the meadows and rice fields.
We can live in happiness forever.
Today, little Korean brother, the guns are firing.
Tomorrow we will sing a new song.

I STAND HERE

I guard my post this evening
At the end of Ben Hai Bridge.
The steady blue current below
Is like a blood vein joining North to South.
Green rice fields reflect in my badge.
Our nation's flag was handed down to us by our loving mother.
Each passing moment reminds me that
My parents and native land

Have entrusted this son with the nation's fate.
Standing before the gusts of wind
And the enemy's front-line,
Son, never forget.
Though seven years have passed
Remember all my advice:
Man your post proudly each evening
For the glory of the motherland.
Though the wind may howl and the rain pour
Keep looking forward.
Word has come over the loudspeaker;
We are to head South.
My beloved home village fades in the distance.
I miss the harvest season
I miss the girls of home
Hair longer than one's outstretched arm.
Now the girls valiantly defend our village.
Hue knows peace and tranquillity;
The Perfume River sings.
My native village knows hunger.
Every night the echoes of Southern gunfire
Tear at my insides.

FROM MY HEART OF HEARTS

The enemy guns thunder
More madly with each passing moment,
Marking the fall of many of my friends;
They will never know life again.
The motherland weeps for them.
How can we possibly surrender?
We are the proud soldiers of the bridge,
Bearers of the Party's teachings.

We must silence the enemy,
Still them like glassy waters.
I stand here, defending factories and farms.
Day and night, they bustle with activity
So the motherland will be blessed in wartime.
I stand here so my sister can attend school,
So our village can ever greet the new year.
I stand here at the demarcation line
Looking South, remembering North.
I am divided like the land.

AFFECTION

My rifle firmly in hand
I cannot leave this land.
I love this land of the bridge's end
Where I have stood guard these seven years.
The pines of Vinh Linh tower upward forever,
I love the rows of folksy houses.
The wind unfurls the Star Flag.
Still, I miss the family hearth.
I picture the road of my native village,
A small lantern shining at each home's gate.
My troops by my side
Bring warmth to my soul.
I wish the country was no longer divided
So we could be together as friends
Enjoying the pure water of Son Nghe
The fishing boats of Phu Xa
Cassava cakes from Ghua Market
Kim mon sweets imbued with the love of old,
The fish of canoes traversing Chau and Hai Thai.
But the Americans and Diem have partitioned us

Here at the Ben Hai River
We, the combatants of the bridge's end,
Remain always here
To thwart the enemy's advance.
Our faith is steadfast
Though by now, it's been seven years
Since husbands and wives, fathers and sons
Have seen each other.
I stand here watching the enemy
Forcing civilians to build bunkers.
Many the age of my mother and father labor at gunpoint.
Infants cry out to be breast-fed,
But the mothers must work.
Often I seethe with rage,
Chafing before the division of this nation.
Month after month, I meet enemy
soldiers. So how can I avoid sorrow?
We are of one blood, one race. Brother,
how can you be such a traitor! The road
you are on is full of blood and sin.

I CANNOT WAIT IN VAIN

My darling, I can't take this anymore.
I only know my little life.
A diamond reveals its full worth
When shining in the darkness,
Inflaming sweet happiness.
I only want to hear poetry as the sun sets;
I promise I will be loving, faithful.
Our laughter will ring out in every direction.
I only want to watch the autumn sunset,

Your heart beating next to mine.
Our renewed life will arrive on the morning wind,
Once the clouds pass by.
I only want a pleasant autumn.
Love is forever and never forgets.
I will receive your love with open arms,
You are a beautiful flower at age twenty.
I only want your heart to belong to me.
Though we all too briefly shared love
It gives me a reason to live.
The water flickers as fish jump,
By fives and sevens.
Baby bird sibs soar above the open sea.
I reach out my arms to embrace my country.
The surf embraces me.
We grew up together, then went our own ways.
One friend fishes these seas night and day;
My memories are like raindrops to the ocean.
Always, my love, I miss your rosy cheeks;
Your boat has docked inside me forever.
Do you remember the quiet evenings
The sunset reflecting on the water
The wind tossing your hair?
The breaking waves laugh in time;
Perhaps the water can measure time.
Please keep track of our memories.
We said good-bye, now we are apart.
The boat has taken my girl home.
That evening my heart writhed in pain.
I love, I suffer.
Her boat still parts the evening waters.
Darling, forget me not.
Be happy during your spring years.

Be sad no longer, lest my heart irreparably break.
Always remember our promises
To be faithful and forever in love.
Our love is truly wondrous;
Our hair will turn gray together.
You smile, your lips blossom with
Hope for tomorrow.
Today, on the border, I take in the horizon;
Believing tomorrow will come.

TO MOTHER

Spring is here, your son writes
To wish mother good health, good cheer,
Happy New Year.
The road of hope that would lead your distant son home
Has yet to be paved.
Spring is here; your son yearns for
His mother and native village.
Buds burst to greet the new year;
Love spreads as the blossoms smile.
Spring is here,
Your boy, dear mother, is now a man.
The North sparkles in the new year
Growing happier as the flowers bloom.
The river below the bridge sings with renewed vigor.
Spring brings food and clothing
New railways
The new year stokes the fire of resistance
But leaves your son far away
For your son clings to his oath.
Spring is here, your son is still here.

Toasting the new year
Though missing his mother and home.
In the spirit of spring, your son writes this letter
Wishing you happiness, Mother.
My life is the army;
You are married to a soldier.
Lying here I miss you,
Aching throughout this winter night.
I cannot contain my desire to come home
As my annual ten-day leave draws near.
Sighing, I count the days,
Pining for each next one to come.
The colder the wind, the more I miss you.
Lying here this winter night, who can I tell all this to?
Midwatch, morning watch...
Sleepless nights pass, each watch grows longer.
Thoughts of seeing you still consume me.
Who can stand this war, this kind of life
I find myself lamenting to the moon.
The more I think about you, the greater my sorrow.
We have missed out on so much.
Friends our age have raised families by now.
I envy them so, husband and wife working side by side each day.
They go to sleep, then awaken to the sight of each other.
They are like pairs of white doves.
While we each go our own lonely way.
I dream the resistance has won peace.
I lie next to you, whispering your name.
But you don't answer me in my deep sleep.
Suddenly the rooster crows in morning watch;

We are both alone again.
My head clears, I again painfully realize
It will be many months before I see you again.
I resign myself to endure to the end,
Until the country is reunified.
So I can come home.

A LULLABY

Days, then months pass;
A year is twelve months, each with thirty days.
You sit, numbering the days.
Fully six years have passed since I left.
That day your rosy cheeks were flush with youth.
Their brightness still warms me.
The good old days lapsed into
Ongoing struggle.
At home, you still try to stay busy
Autumn leaves have fallen six times since I left.
You lean against the door, facing the river
hoping.
You lift your gaze to the rosy clouds overhead.
You look around the yard, hoping
But still, see nothing.
The day I left, I promised
That I would return.
I will keep my promise.
You've lost yourself in tending the rice fields
Since the day I left 'til now.
At home, you are still daily hoping;
Your love is like pink silk.
How can I write all that I think of you?
You are a bird, feathered in lotus petals.

What could be brighter than the glow of us
together?
The greatest love is yours.
As I lean against this light pole during
midwatch,
I gaze at your picture and return your smile;
So sweet is your expression.
Our love is like the sunrise
Shedding light through rosy clouds.
Missing me, you think up some verse;
With this pen, I will jot it down.
I am awkward; I don't know what to say.
How will I finish this letter
My heart is bursting.
Though far apart
The distance does not separate us.
We remain joined
In the spring of our lives.

THE FLUTE

"Last night beside the fire, I stayed up all night.
I made this flute for you, my love.
Until we meet again,
May you see my face each time you play.
Remember our promises to remain forever
faithful.
I can see you playing the flute constantly.
Though far apart, you will
always be waiting for me."

"My love, you joined the army to serve your
country.

Troubled, I yet advised you to defend your native land.
We embrace, oh my dear
Never embrace another.
Please always remember the flute you gave me.
Remember our promises to remain forever faithful.
Though far apart, I will always be waiting for you.
I stand here in the rice fields at day's end;
Mist clouds the horizon.
My little flute melody
Has been carried off by the wind.
It is for the one I love
Miles and miles away.
The rice shouts with glee in the fields
The blooming flowers renew my hope.
I sew this shirt with my love
To send to my faraway soldier.
Though far apart,
I will always be waiting for you
I am always with you."

THE GLAD BLACKSMITH GIRL OF THINH TRUONG

I look up at the tall furnace
Welding fire brighter than the stars;
I look up at the tall furnace
And see the blacksmith girl
Looking up at the stars.
Daily she returns home, satchel in hand
To enjoy a pleasant afternoon,
Still doting on her blacksmith mentor.
See her watch the flowers bloom in the morning

So absorbed in the moment;
She must be scolded by Mom.
Brilliant flames well constantly from the depths of her soul.
These find the tall furnace,
Stoking the welding fire to brighter than the stars
That the blacksmith girl has fixed her eyes on.
She admires the stars as she does the fine welding line
That she so loves.
Day after day, the girl's hands are busy,
For every tomorrow the furnace yields a fresh batch of steel.
She feels happy, watching the country grow stronger
Flourishing like the morning blooms.
At exam time, the girl is a bouquet of fresh roses
The tall furnace makes the future as bright
As the countless stars.

RETURNING NORTH TO VISIT HOME

The dirt road leading home is vermilion red,
Ablaze like my soul.
Wind teases the green rice seedlings
Corn on the hillside sways gently in the breeze.
The banyan tree in front of the coffee shop
Recalls the days when I was young.
The mossy lake with the long bridge
Recalls the evenings spent fishing.
Thatched cottages, bordered by areca and bamboo
Line the banks

Along with jackfruit and banana trees.
The echo of peoples' voices resounds from the empty ferryboat
As the pigeons' coo lengthens.
But the little book of the moment is lost
In a homeland that stands divided,
In the heart of a separated lover
Who grieves for his broken country.
One day of love spared for the motherland
Is worth a hundred years remembering
The roof on one's home.

SPRING IS COMING

Spring is coming, see the beautiful landscape.
Spring is coming in sweet-smelling blossoms.
Merry butterflies alight on peach branchlets
Undisturbed by the wind, they hail spring's arrival.
Spring is coming, my heart grows warm,
I think fondly of my young friend far away
In the spring of her life.
She is like the golden moon rising in the sky.
I remember our love; I cannot forget
For a thousand years, it will be etched on my heart.
I still await the reunion
Of a youthful wife and husband, mother and son.
But out of duty to my country
I remain out here, defending the hamlets and villages.
Spring is coming, millions of people are eager

to share
Golden sentiments.

Spring is coming, I wish you good health, my love.
Please stay fully true to that which you love.
As you add another choice year to the spring of your life,
Bridle your spirit for the country's sake;
So there will be light for the full moon
So the lotus blossoms will be filled with a sweetness
Matched only by our love.
Far from you, my pen is my voice;
Spring is coming, I send my rosy-cheeked lover a kiss.

LOVE

Love bears no grudge.
It is not a butterfly and flower,
Love endures until old age.
Do not trifle with love, or there will be sorrow.
Do not rush love
In order to enjoy it.
Handle love with care;
Be compromising.
Close your eyes, forget about everything.
Calm yourself, listen to the world speak.
Love bears no grudge.
Love is not a quaint flower arrangement.
Don't put on airs; act from the heart.
The price of fleeting joy is an eternal shame,
But in saying so, do not be close-minded.

See yourself as adored by immortals
Lest you age ungracefully,
Finally to decay with the fallen leaves.
May you exalt love.
Be forever faithful; do not trifle with love.
Show the way for the younger generation.
Do not treat romantic love casually,
Lest it consume you. Handle love with care.

TO MY DISTANT LOVER

Today, amid the fresh spring
We are far apart but still one
In the faith of our youth.
I remember your hearty speech and laughter,
The bright moon rising in the East.
Water running downstream past the wild grass.
The peach's freshness kindles my dreams.
Near you, form truly meets shadow
During long nights, yearning for you
I cling to our vows
Though we cannot live as an ordinary couple.
May your faithfulness never wane.
For a hundred years, meditate on the word
"faithfulness."
The letter-lines refresh our memories,
There is so much to remember.
But surely you don't want to dwell on
Our unfinished love, provoking deep bitterness.
I must stop writing for now;
The pen's nib flounders in my tears
My heart can't be stilled...
Together, let us keep our word.

Though the seas may dry up
May we again laugh together.

SONG TO SEW UNIFORMS BY

Our soldiers are exposed to rain and sun.
The rain chills their insides; the sun burns their skin.
From cloth we fashion uniforms;
Our soldiers are resolved to exterminate the enemy.
My guy fights zealously on the battlefield;
Your gal swears to give her all.
Be quick of hand, brothers and sisters!
Looms whir, gunfire crackles through the green forest.
We fashion our hatred into poems.
Gunfire rhymes with the looms' whir.
We exterminate the enemy to the rhythm.
We sew these uniforms with great care,
For the satisfaction of the liberating soldiers.
Be quick of hand, brothers and sisters!
We fashion uniforms; winter draws near.
Proffering fresh new uniforms to you, liberators,
Gladdens our hearts and brings us fulfillment.
We sew uniforms destined for the battlefields;
Be quick of hand, brothers and sisters!

THE SOUTHERNER'S HOMELAND

I hail from the South
Land of blue-green coconut forests,
Land of winding rivers

My homeland is a stranger to hardship.
But after nine years of animosity,
I am determined to carry on the struggle
Until peace and happiness can be heard in
Singing birds returning home,
Golden rice rustling in the paddies,
Boat wakes splashing on glad rivers,
The wind carrying the rower's song.
But how can the South Vietnamese
Under enemy rule
Be so full of song?
Hands covered with our blood
Their hamlets sadly silent,
Writhing pitifully in the hate.
The people struggle for a single nation;
The future holds unity.
North and South will share the same flag.
Tomorrow we will sing a thousand songs
together.
The South is shimmering rice fields,
Abundant blue waters.
Listen to the boats rocking, moored happily on
the river.
Troops and civilians live together
The harvest grows more bountiful
With the peace and joy.
For two years, I have fought here in the South;
One day North and South will fight together.
To build a bright tomorrow.
As a bird finds her way above the forest,
The days and months will find
peace in the South.

Warmly dedicated to Comrade Huu T. East Unit. Dedicated to Comrade Huu, on the occasion of his departure for fulfilling his military duties.

My comrade, carry with you a valiant fighting spirit. Be deserving of your charge: a pioneer in the People of Vietnam's Army.

T. East, April 8, 1965
Viet Huong Cooperative
Ward Phang
District of Dien Bien
Lai Chau City

FOOTNOTES

The author of the poem (one of Lt. Nghia's friends) is standing guard at the Hien Nghi Bridge, which crosses the Ben Hai River, the demarcation line established in 1954 to separate North Vietnam and South Vietnam. The actual name of the bridge is the Hien Nghi Bridge. The author of the poem refers to the Ben Hai River, which the bridge crosses.

The arrival of spring coincides with the (lunar) New Year for the Vietnamese. There are no "I" and "you" pronouns in Vietnamese. The translation of this poem seeks to capture the fact. It would be non-standard English not to use "I" and "you," which are used throughout the other poems. The author again is taking the role of his wife. The poem is written from the perspective of a girlfriend back home, sewing uniforms for her soldier boyfriend.

www.ingramcontent.com/pod-product-compliance
Lightning Source LLC
LaVergne TN
LVHW010646110826
845149LV00014B/2972

* 9 7 9 8 9 9 0 5 2 4 6 2 0 *